History of Philosophy I

UNI SLOVAKIA series
Volume 11

History of Philosophy I
From Heraclitus to the Sophists

Michal Zvarík

Bibliographic Information published by the Deutsche Nationalbibliothek

The Deutsche Nationalbibliothek lists this publication in the Deutsche Nationalbibliografie; detailed bibliographic data is available in the internet at http://dnb.d-nb.de

The publication of this book is part of the project Support for Improving the Quality of Trnava University (ITMS code 26110230092) — preparation of a Liberal Arts study program, which was supported by the European Union via its European Social Fund and by the Slovak Ministry of Education within the Operating Program Education. The text was prepared at the Department of Philosophy, Faculty of Philosophy, Trnava University in Trnava.

Design and Layout: © Jana Sapáková, Layout JS.
Printing: VEDA, Publishing House of the Slovak Academy of Sciences

ISSN 2366-2697
ISBN 978-3-631-67464-2
E-ISBN 978-3-653-06653-1
DOI 10.3726/978-3-653-06653-1

© Peter Lang GmbH
Internationaler Verlag der Wissenschaften
Frankfurt am Main 2016

All rights reserved.

Peter Lang Edition is an Imprint of Peter Lang GmbH.
Peter Lang – Frankfurt am Main · Bern · Bruxelles · New York · Oxford · Warszawa · Wien

All parts of this publication are protected by copyright. Any utilisation outside the strict limits of the copyright law, without the permission of the publisher, is forbidden and liable to prosecution. This applies in particular to reproductions, translations, microfilming, and storage and processing in electronic retrieval systems.

This publication has been peer reviewed.

www.peterlang.com

Contents

	Introduction More or Less Protreptic		7
1.	Heraclitus of Ephesus		13
	1.1	*Logos* and Unawakened	17
	1.2	Harmony of Contrasts	21
	1.3	Criticism of Cognitive Abilities	27
2.	Parmenides and Zeno		31
	2.1	Prooimion and Ways of Knowledge	33
	2.2	The Nature of Being	38
	2.3	The Way of the Two-headed	42
	2.4	Zeno of Elea	44
3.	Empedocles		47
	3.1	The Principles	49
	3.2	Cosmogony and Zoogony	52
	3.3	Perception and Knowledge	54
	3.4	The *Purifications*	57

4.	Anaxagoras		59
	4.1	Basic Principles	60
	4.2	Sensory Perception and Cognition	65
5.	The Presocratic Atomists		67
	5.1	Atoms and Void	68
	5.2	Knowledge and Cognition	70
	5.3	The Ethics of Democritus	76
6.	The Sophists		81
	6.1	The Historical Context of Sophists	82
	6.2	Protagoras of Abdera	84
	6.3	Gorgias	89
		6.3.1 Thesis I: "Nothing is"	91
		6.3.2 Thesis II: "Even if it exists it is incomprehensible to man"	92
		6.3.3 Thesis III: "Even if it is comprehensible, it surely cannot be expressed or communicated to another"	94
	6.4	*Physis* and *nomos*	95

List of Abbreviations	100
Bibliography	101

Introduction More or Less Protreptic

Despite the fairly widespread decline of philosophy's reputation today, no one seriously doubts that its birth in the Greek environment more than 2,600 years ago marked a turning point in history that gradually crystallised into one of the pillars of European culture and education. The year 585 BC is considered the official "birth year" of philosophy, when a solar eclipse occurred as predicted by Thales of Miletus in the Ionian city located on the west coast of present-day Turkey. According to tradition, Thales of Miletus was the first philosopher ever. Since then, philosophy increasingly emancipated from myth as a peculiar way of thinking, it became a means of human reflection of him/herself, nature and its phenomena, or deities and religion. It gives humankind a substance and means of criticism, clarification and explanation of causes, and it increasingly became a topic and problem of how we can know something and what causes us to be wrong. This textbook aspires to present the reader with at least a small section of this story.

This approach to history has important implications nowadays. We often view the past as a history of mistakes and the present as an epoch that has already managed to largely cope with age-old prejudices and grievances against the truth or the human ethos. From this perspective, exploring the history of philosophy may seem an unnecessary and impractical undertaking. But the task of philosophy consists in asking questions, disputing the established truths that are accepted uncritically rather than screened with responsible criticism, and philosophy's role in this regard has not lost anything of its topicality. On the contrary, it appears that this is one of the moments that is timeless in our culture, rendering it specific in history. Philosophy does not seek only to provide alternative and uncomfortable opinions. Philosophy also seeks standpoints that may be supported with reason and arguments. Such standpoints often become uncomfortable due to the fact that they make us uncertain, disrupt our normal ways of thinking, and affect very sensitive and painful places. Plato and Aristotle believed that philosophising was born of wonder or amazement (*thaumadzein*), and Aristotle pointed out that in the state of amazement our ignorance is revealed to us, and therefore the will and willingness to search for truth. But amazement is no innocent passion that only opens up the unknown before us. In ignorance, we may experience the nothingness of untruths that we previously have not admitted as untruths; amazement may therefore disrupt our customary attitudes.

This textbook is only a short introduction to the history of philosophy, which, as a philosophical discipline, is a part of this undertaking. This may be clarified by reference to the objectives this text seeks to attain. The first function is undoubtedly a doxography, which literally means a "description" or "making a list of opinions" of past philosophers. We must view the history of philosophy as a discipline, an original examination of the performance of thinking in the past, rather than as a set of contained precepts about what this or that philosopher said. We examine the performance of thinking mainly because this is for us the real question, the riddle that we are trying to solve, thus breaking out of our present ignorance about the past. Doxography is not a new discovery and philosophers have devoted efforts to it virtually since the discipline's inception. Often, however, they followed their own objectives and sought confirmation of their own opinions in their predecessors, or they attributed their own views to them. The present role of doxography is thus to clean the original view of philosophers of impurities and misinterpretations that were to some extent the result of the absence of appropriate methods of historical research.

For this reason the history of philosophy needs a special approach, a "dialogue" with the past. Philosophical views have their own specific historical contexts, and it requires that we depersonalise our current attitudes and attempt to view philosophical problems "through the eyes of the other," that is, from the perspective of the historical framework in which they were developed. One may argue against this method and it is a relevant (philosophical) question whether this claim can be fulfilled at all. Of course, achieving an absolute certainty that our interpretation is indeed the only true one is not possible.

The importance of the history of philosophy is not exhausted only in an effort for the best possible doxography, but it overlaps with the present as well. It clarifies for us what philosophy means and has meant; it draws attention to a human as a changeable being living in history, on who directs history and simultaneously is directed by it. Many major philosophical figures do not belong only to the past in the strict sense, but are discovered anew and inspire new answers to current issues. Finally, based on the aforementioned, we may conclude that the history of philosophy has an important role in the criticism of the present and when present prejudices are accepted without a shadow of doubt. In historical-philosophical investigations, current bias often comes to the surface, which "compartmentalises" the past according to its own schemes and gives the past meanings and attitudes that it may not have. On the contrary, looking into the past forces us to find the living roots of its opinions and experience, not in order to reject it, but primarily to understand it. Here, we are at "risk" of finding a peculiar "truth" in an ancient mistake and relativising and suspending validity of truths of today.

Of course, these objectives go far beyond the possibilities and scope of the present text, in part because of its limited space. Therefore, our objectives naturally have to be considerably more modest. This in itself does not pose much of a problem, because we do not claim to provide more than a preliminary and rather basic introduction to the Pre-Socratic period thinkers when philosophy obtained its first contours of historical development. In this situation, less is sometimes more. The problems related to the thinking of individual philosophers is in practice much more complex, as the penetration into such matters assumes that the reader already has some background of basic knowledge and understands philosophical terminology. For this reason the presented text does not take and cannot take into account all the plurality of views on the issues discussed. Limited space presented a problem during the preparation of this text, in such a way that I had to decide between two mutually exclusive options: either focus on pre-Socratic philosophy in its more significant historical extent, or simply omit a number of important authors and devote the remaining scope to the "chosen few." In the former possibility, in my opinion, there may be a certain vagueness and therefore possible incomprehensibility of substance, while the latter approach may be criticised for its arbitrariness of selection. As suggested by the subtitle, *From Heraclitus to the Sophists*, I chose the latter approach, and it must be admitted that the selection was preferential, without any fair rule. I believe that the result of this decision is a better penetration into a certain way of thinking. Therefore, the reader will not find important topics of Pre-Socratic research, such as the meaning of the myth, the historic context of philosophy, representatives of Milesian and Pythagorean thinking, etc.

A brief comment is also required regarding working with the literature. The English translations of the surviving fragments and testimonials were primarily drawn from the two-volume work by Daniel W. Graham, *The Texts of Early Greek Philosophy*. In references, I generally follow the sign convention established by H. Diels and W. Kranz, which was also used by Graham. Unless I draw from a different translation, I specify this fact in the relevant footnote. A general exception to this procedure is only with regard to the fragments of Heraclitus. Their translation comes mainly from the work of Ch. H. Kahn, *The Art and Thought of Heraclitus,* and for clarity I use the author's designation of the fragments in Roman numerals.

1. Heraclitus of Ephesus

Heraclitus of Ephesus (540 – 480) is probably the most original, but also one of the least accessible among the Pre-Socratic philosophers. He has a reputation as an aristocrat, a staunch enemy of democracy, and abuser of the crowd, referring to the famous saying by Bias that "many are worthless, good men are few" (22 B 104, LIX). Even the doxography of his thinking presents a fairly ambivalent image, often laced with anecdotes caricaturing his personality more pronounced than usual compared to other thinkers of this epoch, although often based directly on his work. In contrast, Heraclitus was a major inspiration; in some aspects he was followed by, for example, the Stoics, sceptics, and his contribution was recognised even by Early Christian thinkers.

The treatise by Heraclitus, with the attributed name, *On Nature,* raises ambivalent responses as well. Even if, in comparison with earlier authors, we have disproportionately more fragments available, their interpretation is not altogether simple and has aroused controversies from the times of ancient doxography until the present. The cause is an unusual and engaging literary style, for which he earned the nickname, Dark (*Skoteinos*). According to the Peripatetic school, his writing was a prime example of how not to compose philosophical writings. In contrast, according to Diogenes Laertius, Socrates was reportedly heard to say about the treatise: "The part I understand is excellent, and so too is, I dare say, the part I do not understand; but it needs a Delian diver to get to the bottom of it" (DL II, 22). The style of Heraclitus is characterised by frequent equivoques, contradictory sounding sentences, and there is often confusion about the syntax of sentence relations between words, as Aristotle already complained (A 4). It is disputable as to whether Heraclitus left a comprehensive treatise or rather a set of loosely interlocked aphorisms, and this is naturally related to the eternal problem of the arrangement of individual fragments. We have reasons to believe that the treatise had an intentional, non-random structure, and if it consisted of aphorisms, their order was probably not open.

Yet, the reasons for this method of writing are not purposeless and the answer to the question as to why Heraclitus wrote in such an inaccessible way may be found in his philosophy. In the background of his demanding style, it is possible to observe an effort to faithfully disclose his philosophical experience in confrontation with the divine reality that is – as with Parmenides – hidden and remote for the average person. The central notion is an ambiguous term, *logos,* as a pervasive regularity presented as a hidden, unapparent harmony of opposites. Therefore, Heraclitus' contradictions and the differences in fractions are not a manifestation of his inability to think clearly with a logical consistency, but a coherent intention that is faithfully reflected by *logos*.

Logos is divine and difference between divine and the human point of view is as similar to the difference between an adult and a child:

> "A man is called childish by a deity, just as a child by a man" (B 79).
> "Human nature does not have insight, while divine nature does" (B 78).[1]

For this reason, it may not be incorrect to allege that mode of Heraclitus' expression is not far from that of an oracle, which provides people with the divine. But an oracle does not present things clearly: "The Lord whose oracle is at Delphi neither reveals nor conceals, but gives a sign" (B 93). The divine that governs and concerns all things is beyond human capability and exceeds them, and in this regard it is naive to usurp its unique assump-

---

1   English translation adapted from Graham, 2010.

tion and insertion into the general framework of human reasoning. R. Kočandrle expressed this concisely: "The sign '*semainei*' is a more adequate expression of *logos* or *physis*, because it is not a conceptual and defining assumption so typical of European thinking, but a legacy and revelation" (2008, 257).

Regarding the expressive aspect of the treatise of Heraclitus, it must be pre-emphasised that contrariety is not only a principle organising the world into a harmonious unity, but also a principle of uniform and comprehensive understanding. Yet, individual contrarieties do not stand exclusively against each other as opposite detached poles; they mutually penetrate and cross. Therefore, Heraclitus often uses chiasmus, a figure of speech, by which he arranges individual words "crosswise" to illuminate interdependent meanings. An example of chiasmus may be found in the Fragment B 53:

> "War is father of all and king of all;
> and some he manifested as *gods*, some as *men*;
> some he made *slaves*, some *free*" (emphasis Kratochvíl).

Here, chiasmus is found in the following form:

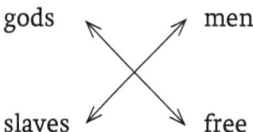

The meaning of chiasmus, therefore, stands that gods are free, while men in comparison to gods are slaves (Kratochvíl 2006, 60-61).

1.1 *Logos* and Unawakened

Today it is quite generally accepted that the treatise of Heraclitus begins with the following words:

> "Although this account (*logos*) holds forever, men ever fail to comprehend (*axynetoi*), both before hearing it and once they have heard. Although all things come to pass in accordance with this account, men are like the untried when they try such words and works as I set forth, distinguishing each according to its nature and telling how it is. But other men are oblivious of what they do awake, just as they are forgetful of what they do asleep" (B 1, I).

The treatise begins by defining the relationship between *logos* and humankind. Humans do not understand *logos*, despite the fact that they constantly face it. Here, we briefly turn our attention to the actual words, *logos* and *axynetoi*. *Logos* is especially true speech, but also a word, a law, and last but not least, a measure or a ratio (Kočandrle 2008, 267). *Logos* retains all of these meanings as diverse shades of the same. *Logos* is characterised by being practically a word or speech, which speaks out as an active regularity. As regularity and speech is common to all (*xynon*), it is the *one* (B 50, XXXIV) with which we all encounter as active.

The conclusion of the fragment reminds us that humans are commonly referred to in *logos* as sleeping, and elsewhere Heraclitus points out: "The world (*kosmos*) of the waking is one and shared, but the sleeping turn aside each into his private world" (B 89, VI). Compared to B 1, we find here a certain shift: in the previous case, humans were vigilant as well as sleeping at the same time, but in both cases it deludes them what they do. In contrast, fragment B 89 distinguishes humans as awake and sleeping, the dividing line between them is created on the basis of awareness of their relationship to *kosmos*. Note that it bears a key characteristic of *logos*, and that it is common. The term *kosmos* does not need to imply only the meaning "world," but also (and perhaps especially) "ordering."[2] The Text B 1, therefore, varies little in a different context which fragment B 89 does not contradict, but rather develops its meaning. Ordinary humans, even when they are awake, are in relation to *logos* as sleeping: they live, so to speak, "in their world," "like in a dream" of their own fantasies and assumptions. In contrast, the wakeful in the context of B 89 are

---

2 This translation is also used by Kahn, 2001. For the origin and evolution of the concept of *kosmos* in presocratic philosophy, see Appendix I in Kahn, 1960.

characterised by an explicit relationship to *kosmos*, they experience it consciously as a common *reality* for all, as opposed to the dreaming ones who "are at odds with that with which they most constantly associate. And what they encounter every day seems *strange* to them" (72 B, V, emphasis M.Z.).

We are thereby converging to the meaning of the expression *axynetoi*, which might be translated as "those who fail to comprehend" or "are out of touch." But this is a complex equivoque referring to what is common, *xynon* and therefore common to all, *logos*. As Heraclitus suggests: "Not comprehending (*axynetoi*), they hear like the deaf. The saying is their witness: absent while present" (B 34, II). Although speech, *logos*, speaks to everyone, even if heard by humans, they act as if they were deaf to it. Comprehension and common *logos* are connected to such a degree that the absence or deficiency of one immediately implies the absence of the other.

The critique of Heraclitus regarding the current approach to reality shows a great sensitivity to its structure. In particular, while for the wakeful *logos* is the only reality, for the average person it is *strange* (B 72, V). But the strangeness of *logos* does not imply only that a mind does not accept it as consciously awake, but especially the fact that he/she may consider it a mistake, something unreal, even if he/she has encountered its adequate interpretation. Instead, a human trusts his/her own opinions (B 17, IV). An interesting question is why people prefer false opinions to the very reality. One of the reasons for the attractiveness of this belief lies in the structure; we may define both as negative, i.e. in relation to *logos*, in which it is absent, and positive, as some resemblance of veracity:

> "Although the account (*logú*) is shared (*xynú*), most men live as though their thinking were a private possession" (B 2, III).

We should not lose sight of the similarity of these lines with Fragment B 89. Indeed, there is only one world and one *logos*, but most people are living in their own fictional world and reflection. Our opinion, therefore, carries a certain orderliness, *cosmos*, and "harmony," which appears to be true, and thus allows for the concealment of true speech. The greatness of Heraclitus lays in the revelation of that fact, regardless of whether we understand it adequately or not; it has for us a meaning, that we are always able to understand it in some way. It is never a total chaos for us, but we always organise it by our "thought." However, there is a certain tension between fictional thinking and the understanding of reality: reality exceeds ordinary opinions and is beyond their framework of organisation, it appears therefore as something meaningless. The fact remains that, compared with reality, *sub specie* deity are false and meaningless individual opinions.

1.2 Harmony of Contrasts

Logos is divine and influences all, it is all pervasive. Therefore, the world is not chaotic, but orderly and lawful, but its regularity acquires the paradoxical nature of a conflict arising between the opposites. Harmony and argument are identical for Heraclitus; there is no arrangement without tension between contrasts, and contrasts that would obviously not organise reality coherently. Thus, contrasts within the whole of reality actually perform several key functions: firstly, contrast is the basic organising relationship, grasping, by which *logos* speaks out, as suggested in a relatively concise form by the Fragment B 10 (CXXIV): "Graspings (*synapsies*): wholes and not wholes, convergent divergent, consonant dissonant, from all things one and from one thing all;" secondly, contradictions enable the whole of reality, but also its individual and various parts, which were endowed with an understandable meaning; and thirdly, contrasts give rise to creation, destruction, and any change.

1. The nature of contrasts as a determining connection is clarified by Heraclitus using the known juxtaposition of bow and lyre:

> "They do not comprehend how a thing agrees at variance with itself; it is an attunement turning back on itself, like that of the bow and the lyre" (B 51, LXXVIII).

Examples of the bow and the lyre are chosen deliberately because of their similar and, at the same time, different features. Both should serve as an indication for understanding the consistency arising from the conflict of opposed differences. They are represented by the opposite poles of a bow or lyre frame. Yet, individual poles create a connection in the form of tension that arises in the bowstring and string. Without the connection between the extremes, it would be impossible to play a sound or shoot an arrow. The symbolism of the harmony of contrasts indicates a higher level here: the bow and lyre have in common not only the fact that they are functional tools based on tension, but they also represent the instruments of Apollo (Kratochvil 2006, 265); still they differ: a bow, since it serves for hunting and killing, is an image of struggle, while the lyre symbolises musical consistency and reconciliation. This expresses the divine relationship speaking out in contrasts.

2. We have already mentioned that, according to Heraclitus, we always understand reality in some way. Reality has thus a meaning for us and it is also made possible and structured by the tension between contrasts: "If it was not for these things, they would not have known the name of Justice (*Diké*)" (B 23, LXIX). Although we cannot be quite sure what specifically the mysterious phrase "these things" refers to, based on the context of other fragments (e.g.: B 102, LXVIII), and by inserting

parts into the relation of contrasts, we can legitimately believe that they are acts of trespassing against the law, and thus lawlessness in a broad sense. The word or concept of the law would have no meaning in the absence of its opposite in the form of lawlessness. Therefore, the meaning is never given without a context shaped by contrasts. Moreover, the same structure underlies human motivations: "It is disease that makes health sweet and good, hunger satiety, weariness rest" (B 111, LXVII).

Affability is only possible due to the fact that there is a contradiction of the unpleasant: we would not feel satisfaction, and in a strict sense, it would not exist for us, in the absence of hunger, i.e. difference, from which it can be distinguished and savoured. Heraclitus thus points out that human life is always immersed in context and it is not possible to sense and feel outside of the framework of contrasts, because they completely penetrate it and determine, as well as structure, our understanding.

3. Heraclitus is often depicted as a thinker of change and a pendant to Parmenides and his concept of unchanging existence. Although one cannot fail to see the differences, there are also important similarities; perhaps the most important is the fact that both thinkers were facing the task of a philosophically articulate reality as a consistent and coherent whole. In later interpretations of Heraclitus, the emphasis on change is so pro-

found that unity, which is constitutive for it, ends up as a background interest. An example is the popular textbook quoting of the statement, "everything flows" (*panta rhei*), which naturally implies the conclusion that nothing lasts. This attitude probably originated in Plato, where the phrase, "you cannot step into the same river twice" (cf. *Crat.* 401d-402a)[3], is also attributed to Heraclitus.

But to understand Heraclitus' concept of change, we have to put it into a broader context. Let us mention the most important fragments dealing with this problem:

"Into the same rivers we step and do not step, we are and we are not" (B 49a).

"As they step into the same rivers, other and still others waters flow upon them" (B 12, XCIII B).

"Sea pours out ⟨from earth⟩, and it measures up to the same amount [*logon*] it was before becoming earth" (B 31, XXXIX).

"All things are requital for fire, and fire for all things, as goods for gold and gold for goods" (B 90, XL).

"The ordering (*kosmon*), the same for all, no god nor man has made, but it ever was and is and will be: fire ever living, kindled in measures and in measures going out" (B 30, XXXVII).

---

[3] English translation by C. D. C. Reeve, from Cooper, 1997.

Fragment B 49 indicates that in every change, existence and non-existence are both present. A soul entering a river is not the same as before it entered, because it finds itself in the flow of time. The past soul is no longer, but the present soul exists. But also the river is not the same, because it also changes over time. However, it is wrong to infer that because of change, there is nothing permanent: for the soul to change, it must retain something permanent on top of which changes may take place. But a river also has the permanent form of the riverbed where the "waters flow upon them."

Heraclitus presents change against the background of a unity of contrasts, according to which everything starts from One *et vice versa*. The first striking contradiction in these fragments comprises of fire and water, which may indicate an inspiration in the Milesian context of thinking about natural phenomena:[4] "Cold warms up, warm cools off, moist parches, dry dampens" (B 126, XLIX). The contrast of fire and water also points to another major difference: while the fire is featured in the singular, we encounter the river in the plural (Kratochvil 2006, pp. 183-184). Therefore, the text states that as change is not without stability, it presupposes the *contrast of unity and plurality*. The individual elements are not equivalent, but – as pointed out by the context – fire, referring to what is

---

4 In the available sources, however, Heraclitus does not mention any of the Milesian *physiologoi*.

common and unified for all, carries, so to speak, a higher dignity than water.[5] The comparison to gold is not only an allusion to its richness, but also the common *logos*, both in terms of what is common and unified to all, as well as in the sense of measure (*metron*). Each product has its own "measure" in the form of a price to be paid in gold to allow the exchange to take place. Both dimensions can be found highlighted in the famous saying about the *cosmos*, which is "the same," it is identified with fire and ignites and dies out according to measure.

At the background of this global change, we also must see Heraclitus' understanding of creation and destruction. Things arise by the decline of fire, allowing them to arise. In contrast, ignited fire destroys things, they are transformed into fire. Above each formation and destruction remains something in common, and that is the measure. As C. Osborne summarises: "Thus Heraclitus can maintain that the discontinuity in the changes observed in the world is structured by a system of measured proportion, the *logos* that ensures that what we have after the change is ... the same value: it is measured to the same *logos*" (Osborne 2003, pp. 100-101).

---

[5] This is also evident from Heraclitus' reflections on the nature of soul: "A man, when he gets drunk, is led by a beardless lad, tripping, knowing not where he steps, having his soul moist." (B 117, CVI). A moist soul makes a man intoxicated and thus he looses clarity. In contrast: "The dry soul is the wised and best." (B 118, CIX).

1.3 The Criticism of Cognitive Abilities

Turning attention to the status of a human within the order of the whole is undoubtedly one of Heraclitus' great merits. There is a present distance between humans and God; a human and God are opposites, just like a part and a whole. We have already mentioned that *logos* concerns all things, it penetrates all, and everything happens according to it. But in opposition to the aforementioned, and in a critical tone towards different teachings, Heraclitus notes: "Of all those whose accounts (*logús*) I have heard, none has gone so far as this: to recognize what is wise (*sofon*), set apart from all" (B 108, XXVII). The wise is separated in the sense of the divine that for a human is as inaccessible and cannot be made into an object. Heraclitus thus opens up the problem of the relationship between the apparent and unapparent – an unapparent divine harmony, which exceeds an apparent harmony, is a way for a human to encounter things and understand them (B 54, LXXX).

Due to the human distance from the wholeness of reality, it is not quite right to talk about Heraclitus' gnoseology in a positive sense: knowledge presupposes an object that is firmly defined, but Heraclitus' intent is in the direction of grasping a whole that transcends human possibilities: "If one does not hope for the unhoped for, one will not discover it, since it is undiscoverable and inaccessible" (B18).[6] This experience forms the fundamental basis consisting of the human situation, the scarcity of which in relation to the overall arrangement must be necessarily accepted. The path to it then leads through exploring oneself (B 101, XXVIII). It is not possible to obtain a solid knowledge, but rather an understanding of the "signs" through which *logos* speaks.

This focus on the situation and context of human understanding gives space to the criticism of cognition, namely the question of whether and to what extent our abilities allow us to properly grasp the context. In this regard, Heraclitus' fragments focusing on sensory evaluation and a criticism of "polymathy" (*polymathia*) are interesting. For Heraclitus, polymathy has a negative meaning: "Much learning does not teach understanding. For it would have taught Hesiod and Pythagoras, and also Xenophanes and Hecataeus" (B 18, XVIII). Nevertheless, he does not reject the knowledge of many things, rather the opposite: "Men who love wisdom must be good inquirers into many things indeed" (B 35, IX). Among these fragments, this is merely an apparent paradox. Heraclitus does not distinct himself only from the tradition of major thinkers, but especially from an approach that delivers or absorbs much individual knowledge, lacking a proper connection. Individual knowledge is only something apparent; it needs to be understood in the context of unapparent harmony. "Understanding"

---

6   English translation by Graham, 2010.

in the first and a "love of wisdom" in the second fragment indicate that this context is *logos* as a harmony of contrasts.

A similar ambivalence is also found in his texts focused on sensory perception:

> "Whatever comes from sight, hearing, and learning from experience: this I prefer" (B 55, XIV).
>
> "Poor witnesses for men are the eyes and ears of those who have barbarian souls" (B 107).[7]

A positive assessment of the senses by Heraclitus probably arose from the fact that they unite us with facts and thus enable experience. Their advantage is primarily in their ability to distinguish between individual and partial.[8] Therefore, Fragment 107 does not reject sensory perception as such, but warns of its inadequacy. The senses by themselves are unable to provide an acceptance of reality. On the contrary, we always organise what we see into some context of our private assumptions. Of note here is the use of the term "barbarian soul:" "A barbarian in the historical sense is one who does not share a common language, common traditions and common frameworks of experience" (Kratochvil 2006, 272). A barbarian soul is thus a reference to *axynetoi* unable

---

7 English translation by Graham, 2010.
8 So may indicate fragment B 7 (CXII): "If all things turned to smoke, the nostrils would sort them out."

to recognise a common *logos*. Heraclitus takes a comprehensive approach in affirming the whole, based on the recognition of the basic context through the involvement of different senses and a unifying understanding that the whole is not simply given, but cultivates the soul through introspection.

2. Parmenides and Zeno

In the history of thought, the founder of the Eleatic school, Parmenides (540/515 – 470/449), represents a radical turnaround. The examination of *physis* is no longer in the centre of interest, but attention is turned to more abstract problems of existence and thinking, predisposing new horizons of questions that are asked by later thinkers. Subsequent philosophy could either follow Parmenides, or go against him, but never without him. Since he explicitly asks the question about existence, he is rightly regarded as the first ontologist. But we should not forget that the distinction of philosophical sub-disciplines is of a later date, and for the Greeks, problems related to existence inevitably implicated diverse questions of knowledge practically into one package. And so we see that the fundamental distinction of areas of existence, and the phenomenon established by the Eleatic philosophy, have necessary implications for the criticism of cognition, where we may encounter a dismissive attitude towards experience and its ability to report truthfully. Parmenides' thought, moreover, makes the first steps towards the discovery of the rules of formal logic, because here he explicitly echoes that thinking has to follow certain rules, which exclude the opposite claims.

Several fragments were preserved of Parmenides' works and poems, which were later ascribed traditionally the title, *On Nature*. The treatise had originally more than 800 verses, from which about 160 were preserved. Interpretation is not quite simple, however, especially since they are not written in prose that would be more appropriate for the presentation of Parmenides' abstract thought. Moreover, it is possible that the novelty and richness of the presented philosophical experience forced Parmenides to stretch the possibilities of contemporary language, because the adequate and customary terms for its expression were not yet available. On the contrary, it was here where possibilities for an improved and more thorough specification of terms appeared. However, complications are caused by the fact that we may not quite neglect how we determine the order of fragments. The poem consisted of the Prooimion and another two parts. In the first of these, the goddess Dike reveals to Parmenides "the unshaken hearth of persuasive Truth," where we find the ontological and epistemological core, and in the second part we encounter the opinions of mortals concerning the cosmological order.

2.1 Prooimion and Ways of Knowledge

Prooimion (28 B 1), which is in its style not too far from a religious revelation (KRS 317), or initiation into the mysteries (Palmer 2012), is strikingly different from the rest of the text, where we encounter more factual reasoning, although clouded by hexametre. Here, Parmenides, who is driven by "the well discerning mares," recounts his journey to the goddess of justice, Dike, on which he is led by sun maidens who, upon leaving the abode of Night, remove their veils. The fact that Parmenides, who by all appearances, needs to point out the uncommonness of his statement, which is distant to ordinary human experience, may justify the difference of the introductory part. Therefore, we face a gate separating the way of Day and Night, to which Dike holds the key. The theme of the way is crucial here. The gate serves as a division between the understanding of mortals that is conventional and permeated by deception, and the divine way of Truth: "Since no evil fate sent you forth to travel this way (*for indeed it is far from the track of men*), but Right and Justice" (emphasis M.Z.). The way of Truth is hidden to ordinary human understanding and is revealed only when he leaves the way of Night, i.e. to be guided by maidens, who by removing their veils show themselves as they really are. "Well discerning mares" and "maiden daughters of the Sun" are a metaphor or allegory of a rigorous intellectual inquiry that is exempted from opinion and sensory experience, thus revealing true orderliness. This order is guaranteed by the authority of Dike, who may be seen as a personification of necessity (*ananké*) defining the limits:

> "Come now and I shall tell, and do you receive through hearing the tale, which are the only ways of inquiry for thinking: the one: that it is and that it is not possible not to be, is the path of Persuasion (for she attends on Truth); the other: that it is not and that it is right it should not be, this I declare to you is an utterly inscrutable track, for neither could you know what is not (for it cannot be accomplished) nor could you declare it" (B 2).
>
> "... for the same thing is there for thinking and for being," or alternatively "... for it is the same thing that can be thought and that can be" (B 3).

The passage from fragment B2 was and still is the subject of a controversy that we must at least mention briefly. Dike points out that there are only two original ways that an examination may follow. The way is a metaphorical expression of a line of reasoning (Hussey 2003, 132), which must be ensured by the right starting point. *The first option*, "that it is and is not possible not to be," is the true way according to Dike. In contrast, *the second option*, "that it is not and that it is right that it should not be," is excluded. The decision for the first of the ways stems from the relationship between thinking (eventually knowledge) and existence. There are two options shown here, depending on the translation. Either, thinking and existence have a common object, or thinking and existence are the same.

At the same time, the overlapping of thinking and existence implies that "what-is-not is" is not viable. It is not possible to think about what is not; *thinking must have an object that already exists*. On the contrary, that, what does not exist, cannot be meaningfully thought of and even known. But Parmenides also rejects this line of reasoning because it is contradictory – it forces us to recognise that what does not exist exists at the same time.

> "It is right to say and to think that what-is is, for being is and nothing is not. These things I bid you consider. From this first way of inquiry I withhold you, but then from this one, which mortals knowing nothing wander, two-headed. For helplessness in their breasts directs a wandering mind; and they are borne both deaf and blind, dazed, undiscerning tribes, by whom to be and not to be are thought to be the same and not the same, and the path of all is back-ward turning (*palintropos*)" (B 6).

Parmenides' rejection of "what-is-not is" naturally leads to a rejection of the opinion of so-called double-headed or ordinary people that existence and nonexistence is and is not the same. It thus represents a third option of examination. After a clarification of the unviability of the second way, it is clear that this line inevitably leads to contradictions. Thus, we encounter here a reflection of a certain indiscrimination, an absence of ability to distinguish that understands the statements, "what-is is" and "what-is-not is," without problems as viable options.

> "Never shall this prevail, that things that are not are. But you, withhold your thought from this [third] way of inquiry, nor let habit born of long experience force you along this way, to wield an unseeing eye and echoing ear and tongue. But judge by reasoning (*krinai de logó*) the very contentious examination uttered by me" (B 7).

Parmenides explicitly highlights the close links between sensory perception and the error of the double-headed that stand in stark contrast to differentiation through reason (*logos*). Indeed, we normally relate to reality, phenomenologically speaking, in a natural attitude, in which we uncritically accept things as given and we are used to navigating on the basis of what our senses offer us. Through perception, we constantly persuade ourselves that there is a multiplicity, that things appear and disappear, that we encounter imperfections, consequently with everything that Parmenides rejects in other parts as impossible (B 8, 38-41), because these beliefs assume the defensibility of the paradoxical argument that existing and non-existing at the same time is and is not. The experience, supported by a sensory perception, is therefore misleading, it needs to be suspended, so to speak, and we must turn to distinction by reason alone. But under the fallaciousness of senses, we should not understand phenomena of optical illusions, e.g.: If a rod is put into the water, it seems cracked, although in reality it is not. Parmenides is more concerned with the incompatibility between how reality is given to the senses, and how it is accessible to reason.

This turning away from a conventional approach actually reveals the ontological region of *sui generis*. The contrariety of reason and perception closely corresponds to splitting into the area of existence accessible to thinking, on the one hand, and appereances grasped by perception, on the other. Parmenides, in words reminiscent of Heraclitus, suggests the following:

> "Look at things though absent for the mind present securely: for you will not cut off what-is from clinging to what is, since it is neither scattered everywhere in the world nor combined" (B 4).

Things, which are uncovered solely to reason (*nús*), are not localisable in space, where we could point at them and distinguish them from the rest of "being," as we are naturally accustomed. On the contrary, the object of thinking is grasped outside the field of phenomena, in which, through experience we encounter the multiplicity and changeability of things that separate and combine. The deceptiveness of sensory perception thus lies in the fact that it focuses exclusively on variable appereances. This natural and immediate focus on the side of appearances is the aforementioned way of Night from Prooimion, against which being is veiled.

2.2 Nature of Being

The first part of the poem continues with an explanation and substantiation of the nature of existence resulting from the thesis "what-is is" (B 8): "Only one tale is left on the way: that it is; and on this are posted very many signs, that what-is is ingenerated and imperishable, a whole of one kind, unperturbed and complete."

1. *Being does not change, does not come-to-be, and does not cease-to-be.*

According to Parmenides, being is eternal and cannot come to be or cease to be. Reasoning proceeds dialectically in a sense, i.e. it points out how coming to be and ceasing to be result in contradiction, since they assume the possibility of "what-is-not is" as a viable way:

"Nor ever from what-is-not will the strength of faith allow anything to come to be beside it. Wherefore neither to come to be nor to perish did Justice permit it by loosening its shackles, but she holds it fast. And the decision concerning these things comes to this: it is or it is not. Thus, the decision is made, as is necessary, to leave one way unthought-of, unnamed – for it is not true way – the other to be and to be true."

Hypothetically, there are two options as to how existence could come to be and eventually cease to be. Firstly, if it is came from (or ceased to) nothing, and secondly, in case of change, when it comes to be from (or cease to be to) something else. According to Parmenides, creation from nothing is not possible, because it presupposes the being of "what-is-not," which is an apparent contradiction. This also implies the second option is unverifiable: "Thus it must be completely or not at all." The transformation of one being to another assumes that they differ one from another. But, if they are different, then one must possess something that the other is missing. The paradox is obvious, existence cannot miss anything, because absence, nothing, cannot exist. Since the coming and ceasing to be lead to a contradiction, we must recognise that being is eternal and unchanging.

2. *Existence in itself remains the same, perfect and indivisible*:

> "Nor is it divisible, since it is all alike, nor is there anymore here, which would keep it from holding together, nor any less, but it is all full of what-is. Thus it is all coherent, for what-is cleaves to what-is."

Existence, according to Parmenides, is inevitably one, coherent, and identical with itself, which excludes its divisibility and multiplicity. Here too the argument from consequences is possible. Suppose that being may be separated, and we would thus have to say that it is multiple. In this way we could show that somewhere else there is more of it, and elsewhere less. But if it may be less, then inevitably lacks something, thus we ascribe it a sort of absence. Again, we are led to a contradiction when we ascribe absence to existence. The identity of existence thus ultimately prevents that it could be imperfect; it is perfect, because there is no absence of anything.

Parmenides emphasises the integrity of existence via likening it to a sphere (*sfairos*), because its surface in comparison to its centre is the same everywhere. All points on the surface are "equal" to each other; none of them stands above the other. This image can be confusing at a first glance due to an apparent paradox of the boundedness and boundlessness of being. It is boundless, because it has no beginning and no end. Its definition would need to be inevitably confronted with the thesis "what-is-not is," because we might ask: if being is bounded, what is beyond its borders? This question is meaningless in advance. But relying on the metaphor of a sphere (*sfairos*), Parmenides nonetheless attributes boundaries to being: "Yet, since there is a final limit, it is complete from every direction, like to the mass of a well-rounded ball, equally resistant from the centre in all directions."

The boundedness of being is of a different nature from the boundedness of objects in time and space, since those belong to the area of appearances present to senses. The concept of a boundary must be observed in relation to the concept of necessity (*ananké*). It maintains existence in its entirety, in a "righteous" perfection that is "complete" or "absolute" in the sense that nothing is missing; nothing can be added or taken away from it. Moreover, it is a necessity, which holds being within bounds and prevents it from being something else. Thus, Parmenides points out that being is not accidental; it is essential (Patočka 1996, 126). This, as we have repeatedly mentioned, excludes the possibility of the opposite, which is non-being. From this – again, inevitably – must be concluded that being is one, compact, perfect, and unchanging. The greatness of Parmenides also lies in the discovery that thinking grasping being cannot be random, but must be guided by legitimate rules that are in a sense defined by the being itself, and thus making first steps towards a later formulation of rules of logic.

2.3 The Way of the Two-headed

The passage about the judgement of mortals that, according to the promise of Diké constitutes the second and only scantily preserved parts of the poem, represents Parmenides' cosmology. While Parmenides does not ascribe truthfulness to the judgement of mortals, he grants it a certain *probability*. Already in the first part, the judgement of the two-headed was thematised in that they recognise both ways as viable. Both theses are adopted as fundamental principles in the second part. The thesis, "what-is is," is consistent with the principle of fire, and the contradictory thesis is consistent with the principle of night. This process is controversial at first glance. The goddess offers a concept of world order, which is "completely likely," hence "so that no judgement of mortals will ever surpass you." So the concept presented here does not provide any widely held "public" cosmology and even no opinions of Parmenides' predecessors. On the contrary, it is meant to be original and in its accuracy and plausibility to surpass others. But two-headed mortals approach reality through a natural habit to trust their senses that leads them astray. In this position, we encounter change, multiplicity, and imperfection. These phenomena are fiction in the first part of Parmenides' writings. So, an important question arises: what is the need to create any cosmology when it is necessarily a delusion?

Some interpreters believe that Parmenides denies the fact of what we perceive through the senses, and Aristotle, for example, openly accuses him of incoherence, because in the second part of the poem "[he] is being compelled to follow appearances" (A 24) and depends on perception and multiplicity (Patočka 1996, 138). Parmenides' evaluation of the way of the two-headed may show a great sensitivity to the imperfect human situation. Existence may be grasped only by logos, but it does not apply to observed natural events, where we have no choice and we must rely on our senses.[9] As their subject is always something numerous and changeable, it can never be grasped with clarity and confidence. For this reason, cosmological theories are always doubtful and uncertain. But this does not exclude that some of them are more certain and more likely than others. Thus, Parmenides postulates a scientific principle that theory should be as plausible as possible (Hussey 1997, 123).

---

9   E. Hussey notes that for Parmenides, it is not the senses that are misleading so much, but rather our previous experience that distorts our view, similar to the barbaric soul for Heraclitus (Cf. Hussey, 2003, 138).

2.4 Zeno of Elea

Parmenides' articulation of being is distant from our natural way of relating to reality. The significance of his pupil, Zeno of Elea (about 490 – 430), consists in the formulation of several aporia to defend Parmenides' concept against the objections that could be made out of this position. Only aporia aimed against multiplicity has been preserved for us, and moreover, it is supplemented by a less than clear commentary made by Simplicius that omits many things. We learn about the paradox of movement, especially from Aristotle's attempts to refute them in *Physics*. According to Aristotle (29 A 10), Zeno's contribution lies in the discovery of dialectics as a method that brings to light certain internal contradictions of attitude. But we can see that this was also not totally strange to Parmenides either.

The paradox against multiplicity is as follows:

"If there are many things, they must be as many as they are and neither more or less than that number. If they are as many as they are, they would be limited in number. If there are many things, existing things must be unlimited. For there are always other things between existing things, and again things that are other than those between *them*, and thus existing things are unlimited" (29 B 1).

The aim of aporia is to demonstrate that the assumption of multiplicity is untenable, because a limited number of things is ultimately unlimited. But it is not quite clear what Zeno means by "other things existing between existing things." It is possible that he relies on divisibility to infinity, in which it is necessary to lay down a basic and indivisible unit, from which we could add up a total number of things. Whereas, this unit always consists of other smaller units *ad infinitum*, the claim that things are many is undermined by internal contradictions admitting the limitedness, as well as, the unlimitedness of things.

A similar argument is also used in paradoxes aimed against the movement. The *Stadium*, sometimes called *Dichotomy*, shows that it is not possible to travel a short distance in a limited time. So that a runner may run the entire route, he would have to get to its middle, previously to its quarter, etc. up to *ad infinitum*. As with the aporia on plurality, it is impossible to set a basic unit of distance, as it could be split repeatedly to infinity, which means that the limited length of the track is also unlimited at the same time. Any movement therefore is not possible, because it assumes that it is possible, so to speak, to exceed infinity.

An interesting paradox is that of space, in which Zeno develops negation through infinite regress (*regressus ad infinitum*):

> "For every existing thing ought to be somewhere. But if place is an existing thing, where could it be?

Surely in another place, and that in turn in another, and so on indefinitely" (B 5, Simpl. *In Phys.* 563).[10]

This aporia is based on the difference between things existing in space and space itself. If the existing things exist in something else and space is an existing thing, then it must exist in something else. The argument defending the existence of space thus leads to infinite regress.

---

10 Fragment 25, according to the Graham's edition.

3. Empedocles

Parmenides' work was a major breakthrough that consisted in separating a single, integral, and eternal existence from the area of appearance where we encounter multiplicity and change. This separation naturally evoked controversy and the pursuit of harmony between them. One of the first significant reactions came from the scholar, Empedocles (492 – 432), in whose personality meets the reputation of a major poet, magician ("thaumaturge"), physician, politician, and soothsayer. He came from Acragas (Argigentum), a Greek colony in Sicily, supposedly from a wealthy family, and he could afford to pay a dowry to the Acragas' maidens. He is also attributed as having performed miracles, exceptional healing deeds, and pro-democratic political activity. Perhaps most interesting is that in the surviving fragments, he declares himself a god who has committed a sin and fallen from a blissful state to a cycle of reincarnation to be purified. This aspect of his work obviously became the target of legends and anecdotes, especially concerning the mysterious circumstances of his death.

For our purposes, it is interesting that Empedocles' fragments point to a Pythagorean influence. In addition, Empedocles draws from Parmenides and responds to Ionian thinking. This tradition attributed two writings, *On Nature,* and, *Purifications,* to Empedocles. The treatise, *On Nature,* is usually characterised as cosmological and cosmogonic writing, which also deals with the ontological and epistemological consequences of Parmenides' thought. In contrast, *Purifications,* should have been more focused on issues of ethics, morals, and religious life. Therefore, based on this distinction, the fragments available to us, incidentally preserved in the greatest number of all Presocratics, were divided into two groups. Many interpreters believe that Empedocles' considerations contained in the treatise, *On Nature,* cannot be completely harmonised with *Purifications* (Ricken, 1999, 33). Other opinions attempt to see accord between them (e.g.Vitek, 2001), but there are also voices with the opinion that in fact Empedocles wrote only one treatise.

3.1 The Principles

The core of Empedocles' thinking forms the doctrine of four elements, also called roots (*rhizomata*), which are mutually aggregated and segregated by the influence of Love (*Filotés*) and Strife (*Neikos*). Like Parmenides, he claims that creation and destruction do not exist, because it is impossible that something was created from nothing, and ceased to exist in nothingness (31 B 12): "There is no birth of any of all mortal things, neither any end of destructive death, but only mixture and separation of mixed things exist, and birth is a term applied to them by men" (B8). Therefore, there must be something eternal and unchanging. In contrast to Parmenides' single being, this function is fulfilled by a number of elements – water, earth, air and fire – which constitute a kind of basic building material, from which all things are formed (KRS, 380-381). What is commonly called the generation and dissolution, coming and ceasing to be, is only a mixing (*mixis*), or aggregation and segregation, of the elements. Empedocles therefore does not deny the existence of multiplicity; on the contrary, any change may happen, because many elements are qualitatively permanent and may be intermixed. Their eternity and divinity is also indicated by Empedocles who compares them to gods (B 6). We see a similar position with other pluralists, Anaxagoras and the atomists, for example.

The actual mixing process is explained by a fitting metaphor of the painting of ceremonial objects: "As when painters decorate offerings, ... when they grasp colourful chemicals with their hands, mixing them in combination, some more, some less, from them provide forms to like all things, creating trees, men, women, beasts, fowls, water-nourished fish, and long-lived gods foremost in honours. So do not let deception overtake your wits that from somewhere else is the source of mortal things" (B 23), i.e., rather than from four elements. This fragment is also interesting as it clarifies the origins of our mistaken assumptions about creation and destruction that consists in negligence of the "microscopic" level of reality. On a painted image, we encounter representations of things that are conglomerates of different colours. These colours are not original, but they are a specific mixture. For example, the mixing of white and black results in grey, but we are no longer able to observe any black or white colour in it. Black and white, if we keep to the spirit of this analogy, literally do not disappear, but we simply cannot perceive them in the mixture. Incidentally, the specific shade of grey is dependent on the balance between the white and black in the mixture. Accordingly, real matter is a mixture of the four elements (water, earth, air and fire) in a certain *proportion*, which we normally do not perceive. For example, if we see a tree, on the "macroscopic" level, we see the wood as a result of the mixing proportion of the elements in a mixture that is indistinguishable to us on the "microscopic" level. The tree may disintegrate or dissolve what we perceive as destruction, but the basic elements that compose the mixture persist.

But a reference to the basic elements, according to Empedocles, is not enough to explain change. Therefore, he constitutes Love and Strife as fundamental cosmic forces standing behind the generation and separation of the four elements. While Love acts as a harmonising force leading to best mixture, Strife leads to separation, differentiation, and conflict. Here, we must add that according to Empedocles, although generation and destruction do not exist of their own accord, he does not completely avoid using them "out of habit" (B 9). Therefore, there is no contradiction in that, if regarding Love and Strife, he notes: "Double is the birth of mortal things, and double the demise" (B 17). By "things" Empedocles does not mean the immortal elements, but their mixtures ("mortal," ephemeral things), which are normally encountered on a macroscopic scale. The actual highlight of dual creation and destruction is important. In fact, it prevents us from understanding Love as the sole cause of "creation" in the meaning of aggregation, and Strife as the sole cause of the "destruction" consisting of segregation.

3.2 Cosmogony and Zoogony

The reasons for this notion of Love and Strife are clarified when we focus on Empedocles' cosmic cycle. It is these forces that stand in the background and through them he explains a cosmogonic and zoogenic processes. According to one line of interpretation, this cycle can be divided into four phases. The first phase is characterised by the total dominance of Love which forms a perfect sphere, *Sfairos*, from the elements. In *Sfairos*, the individual elements are so mixed that they are indistinguishable from one another (A 41). In the second, incidentally, referred to by Aristotle as the "contemporary" phase (A 42), Strife starts to manifest and through a vortex (*diné*), it disrupts *Sfairos*, whereby the cosmos is formed and consequently zoogony takes place. The third phase is an all-out dominance of Strife causing a complete separation of different elements in the vortex, and thus the destruction of the cosmos. Finally, the fourth phase begins by the manifestation of Love, which gradually gains superiority over Strife, so that everything heads toward the creation of a new cosmos and later to the re-creation of *Sfairos*.

An alternative interpretation points out that Strife or Love are not totally dominant and therefore, in the case of domination by Strife, the complete separation of the individual elements does not occur. The result is that there is only one cosmogony (Parry, 2012).

Both Love and Strife share in generation and dissolution: Love causes the dissolution of "mortal" things by increased mixing of the elements, leading to fulfilment in the formation of *Sfairos*. By contrast, via the influence of Strife, things do not need to be segregated solely into individual elements, but into mixtures with a lower or less perfect mixing ratio. Finally, it is Strife that causes the destruction of *Sfairos*, but by doing so, it also allows *cosmos* to arise, while the opposite is true for the influence of Love.

Zoogony, the process by which all living creatures are formed and evolved, is also a part of the cycle. This part of Empedocles' doctrine is very attractive for the modern mind, because a predecessor of the theory of evolution is observed in it; although one should avoid such prepossessing precipitance. At the beginning of zoogony, we find a quite bizarre situation where individual organs and limbs are separated and do not form any coherent organisms: "As many heads sprouted without necks, and bare arms strayed deprived of shoulders, and eyes wandered alone, bereft of foreheads" (B 57). Through the influence of Love, these scattered bodies begin to merge and combine, forming diverse, though still bizarre bodies: "Many creatures grew with faces or chests before and behind, man-faced oxkind, and in turn there rose up ox-headed mankind, mixed here from man, there from woman-nature, outfitted with shadowy limbs" (B 61). Although, under the influence of Love, various organs desire for interconnection in a certain body; a scarcity of Love causes many links lead to the formation of imperfect and ineffective animals that are unable to provide their own survival and reproduction. At a later stage, those animals survive that have well adapted organs and limbs and are able to multiply, above all.

3.3 Perception and Knowledge[11]

By means of the four elements, Empedocles attempted to explain the functioning of sensory perception and thinking, in which his medical knowledge can also be observed. Perception is to function, according to Theophrastus' comment, on the basis of similarity, which is usually interpreted in two ways. The first is associated with the fact that things are composed of elements that emit effluences with a specified shape. These effluences then enter the pores or pathways (*poros*) of the sensory organs. The pore shapes of the individual senses differ from each other and thus admit only those effluences that are shaped for transition through the pores (cf. A 86). The second is associated with perception on the basis of the commonality of perceived and sentient elements: "By earth we behold earth, by water water, by aether divine aether, but by fire blinding fire, by affec-

---

11 Cf. Vítek 2001, 290-292.

tion affection, strife by dreadful strife" (B 109). In a similar manner, Theophrastus comments on Empedocles' characterisation of eyesight:

> "In trying to explain the nature of the sight, he says fire is inside the organ, and outside it water, earth, and air, through which what is fine passes just as the light of lantern. There are alternating pores for fire and water, of which we perceive white by those for fire, black by those for water, for each fits into corresponding pore. And colours are conveyed to the sight through effluences" (A 86).

According to Empedocles even thinking is closely associated with the mixing of the four elements. The elements affect thinking through the mixing ratio in the blood and therefore it is subject to physiological influence (B 105).

Parmenides' contribution to the history of philosophy opened up the question of the reliability of the senses in terms of their ability to convey reality truthfully, and this theme also resonates with Empedocles. The human possibilities to get to know the divine are restricted according to Empedocles, but are not entirely non-existent. One can quest for knowledge corresponding to their level despite the fact that the senses have their limits and we do not perceive directly the different elements contained in mixtures. But our senses do not lie and in recognition of how things are in reality, they are important:

"But come, observe with every device in the way in which each thing is clear: neither hold sight higher in trust than hearing or resounding hearing above the clarities of the tongue, nor let any of the other limbs by which thought has a way be deprived of trust, but think in the way in which each thing is clear" (B 3).[12]

The origin of error lies not in perception itself, but rather in how people further handle it. Their view is not quite comprehensive; they do not devote time and attention to thinking about what their senses offer to them. The threat to true thinking is therefore not the falseness of the senses, but rather conceit:

"For narrow are the devices dispersed over the limbs, and there are many wretched impediments which blunt the thought. Having seen a small part of life, swift to die, men rise and flyaway like smoke, persuaded only of what each has met with as they are driven in every direction, every one claims to have found the whole" (B 2).[13]

People are presumptuous when they do not respect their limitations, such as the shortness of human life and that we only perceive in a limited way – from a perspective

---

12 English translation adapted from Barnes, 1987.
13 Translation by Barnes, 1987, partially adapted according to Graham, 2010.

and never the whole. Nevertheless, humans believe that assumptions learned from observing a part of reality are the knowledge of the whole.

3.4 The *Purifications*

In the *Purifications*, Empedocles puts himself into the position of *daimon*, a god who had to leave the divine beatitude (B 112) because he succumbed to strife and sinned by shedding blood. As punishment, he had to descend to earth and survive here for 30,000 years (three times myriads) in many lifetimes (B 114). Compared with divine existence, earthly life in the flow of reincarnation is miserable (B 118, B 121). During three myriads of years, Empedocles was many things, from a bush to a fish (B 117). In the last phase of reincarnations, *daimons* come into the world as magicians, poets, doctors, and political leaders, and "afterwards they blossom as gods foremost in honours" (B 146). Empedocles' divine origin is suggested by the fact that he himself practiced these professions, by which he completes the cycle of repentance for past sins.

In the *Purifications*, Empedocles is significantly influenced by the Pythagorean tradition, not only by the doctrine of reincarnation, but also by everyday moral prescriptions. This impact is proven by the evident ban on eating beans (B 141). According to Empedocles, the major infractions are the killing and eating of meat that he considers as murder (B 136). The killing and eating of meat is not acceptable due to reincarnation, and the man who infringes this command cannot be confident that he is not eating his brother or father. This criticism has far-reaching consequences, not only because he subjects religious beliefs and misconceptions about gods to the criticism, but also the practical, ritual aspects of religion:

> "The father lifting up his own son in a changed form slaughters him with a prayer in his great folly, and they are lost as they sacrifice the suppliant. But he, not heedful of their rebukes, having made slaughter has prepared in his halls a ghastly banquet" (B 137).

Empedocles' criticism of religion is therefore not merely an abstract rational theology and criticism of public religious misconceptions, but an overall criticism of religious practice, which is based on misconceptions about gods and piety. Greek religion was not a private matter for the individual, as it also had a significant social and political dimension. It was meant to protect the community, to provide peace and order, and to prevent the outbreak of conflicts. But, as Empedocles' criticism suggests, the religious practices of communities is in reality godless because its practices are sinful. Thus, not only in communities does traditional religion miss its objective; on the contrary, it brings Strife to their midst.

4. Anaxagoras

Anaxagoras (circa 500 – 427) came from Clazomene in Ionia, but his influence is mainly associated with Athens. Multiple sources (e.g.: DL II, 12-13) present him as a teacher and friend of Pericles. Therefore, he is known as a representative of the democratic mind-set. In terms of his life, it is interesting that he faced a trial and court of impiety, which can be associated directly with his cosmological views, such as claiming that the Sun is a red-hot stone mass. Doxography attributes to him the prediction of a meteorite fall in Aegospotami, which of course was not possible according to popular understanding at the time. This phenomenon could be seen as confirmation of the view that the heavenly bodies are "fiery stones" (59 A 42). Following accusation and court, Anaxagoras left for Lampsacus, where he was a distinguished man, and where he died.

4.1 The Basic Principles

Anaxagoras' work is also a response to Eleatic philosophy, and its specific contribution consists in the possible polemics with Zeno and in an attempt to incorporate opposition to the interpretation of reality. Generation and destruction do not exist, but as with Empedocles, they are only a mixing and segregation of the basic elements:

> "Coming to be and perishing the Greeks do not treat properly. For no object comes to be or perishes, but each is mixed together from and segregated into existing objects. And thus they should really call coming to be mixture and perishing segregation" (B 17).

These elements, presumably somewhat unfortunately named by Aristotle as *homoiomeres* (homogeneous substances), are characterised by a very particular structure and it was no accident that Anaxagoras called them *seeds*. According to Zeno, the presumption of multiplicity is *contradictio in adiecto*, because it leads to the absurd conclusion that a limited number of things are at the same time unlimited. Anaxagoras, however, does not see any problem in this opinion; on the contrary, through this perspective, it is possible to rationally grasp the nature of reality. Fragment B5 may be viewed as a response to Zeno: "When these things are segregated in this way, we must recognize that the totality is no less and no more.

For it is not possible for there to be more than everything, but all things always remain equal." This formulation is interesting not only because it too obviously resembles Zeno's aporia against multiplicity, which cannot be a coincidence. Its significance is primarily that against the spirit of Zeno's argument, it seeks to demonstrate that the infinity of things that are further divisible to infinity is a kind of constant characteristic of reality as a whole. But this whole of infinity pervades not only the whole of reality, but also each existing thing. This refers to another fragment related to Zeno's line of reasoning:

> "For of the small there is not a smallest, but always a smaller (for what is cannot not be). But even of the large there is a larger; and it is equal to the quantity to the small. And in relation to itself each thing is both large and small" (B 3).

On one hand, this text points out a certain relativity of small and large, as we can always imagine something smaller or larger, but on the other hand, it shows the same common characteristic of small and large, which is that both are infinitely divisible, and so there is an infinite number of them. Another important fact is if something is divided into small parts in any way, there always remains a certain *balance* that prevents us from coming to nothingness. Therefore, divisibility to infinity does not lead to perishing in nonexistence.

Anaxagoras was not philosophising primarily to develop or refute the dialectical arguments, but especially to find a specific uniform and constant rational basis whereby it would be possible to explain multiplicity and change. Divisibility to infinity enabled the imagination of a fundamental particle so little that it escapes our senses, yet always large enough to contain everything in itself, so to speak. *Homoiomeres* have exactly this said function. The specificity of these seeds is characterised by Anaxagoras' short, strange phrase, "everything in everything." This does not mean that a particular thing, composed of homoiomeres, was located in another composite thing, e.g.: "this pen" in "that table" (cf. Hussey, 1997, 166). Each particle in some way reflects the whole *kosmos* as it contains all of its existing qualities, substances, and even contradictions. So each homoiomere contains, for example, metal and wood, white and black, or dry and wet. Because everything exists in everything, particular materials and qualities persist unseparated from each other, thus keeping a certain uniformity of the *cosmos*: "as it was in the beginning, so at present all things are still together" (B 6).

Here we may see the suitability of the selected word "seed," which Anaxagoras presumably based on biological phenomena: in the seed is inherent the whole diversity of the parent, from which nourished the offspring, or parts of the future plant. Therefore, it contains everything that is later nourished from it (Vlastos, 1996, 308). If every element in principle includes all materials and quality contained in the *cosmos*, naturally, the question arises how is it possible that new things are created by their aggregation and segregation? According to Anaxagoras, individual seeds are not completely identical, but they bear the character of which they have the most: "No other thing is like anything else, but each one is and was most manifestly those things of which it has the most" (B 12). The variety of materials that we see with our senses is thus ensured that in each seed some matter or quality is *present* more than others. For example, what we view as timber is a compound homoiomeres in which wood is the dominant substance. Fragment B 10 reminds us of the variety of qualities inherent in the seed:

> "For example, in the same seed there are hair, nail, arteries, sinews, and bones, and although they happen to be invisible because of their microscopic size, as they grow they gradually become distinct. 'For how,' he says, 'would hair come from non-hair and flesh from non-flesh?'"

A very similar line of reasoning is also found in an attempt to explain digestion in a reference by Aetius (A 46), where he points out that the various parts of the body can live off food precisely because the diverse materials that compose our body are present in the diet:

> "For he [Anaxagoras] thought the most puzzling difficulty was how from what-is-not something could

come to be, or how something could perish into what-is-not. For instance, we partake of simple food of one kind, bread and water and from these are nourished hair, veins, arteries, flesh, sinews, bones and other parts. So since this happen, it must be granted that in the food consumed are all these entities, and from these entities all things grow. And in that food are parts productive of blood, sinews, bones, and the rest, which parts are grasped by reason."

Since "everything exists in everything," food that consists of basic seed, must necessarily also contain nutrients for the body. Furthermore, this means that, for example, if a bone is meant to grow, it must also bind new particles containing bone. From this we can conclude that, according to Anaxagoras, it is possible that certain seed is divided so that its part may subsequently merge with another.

In addition to the seed, Anaxagoras introduces another principle, *Reason* (or Mind, *Nous*), whose role is to manage the movement of the *kosmos* and its layout. As the ruling principle, "it exercises complete oversight over everything and prevails above all," and it is characterised by the highest purity and fineness. Reason penetrates all, even though the exception to the rule, "everything in everything," applies to it because if it was not separated from other seeds, it alone would be subject to regulation, and it could not rule (B 12). *Nous* is thus responsible for cosmological and cosmogonic processes. At the beginning, the "aether and air" which "dominated all things" (B 1), formed the original mixture in which the seeds were mixed so that they were indistinguishable. *Nous* then formed the *kosmos*, so that the mass could be put into a whirling motion to start the process of segregation (B 13) leading to the formation of the earth, water, and stone (B 16).

4.2 Sensory Perception and Cognition

Anaxagoras' comments on the process of sensory perception, and the question of knowledge, are also remarkable. Unlike Empedocles, perception according to Anaxagoras functions on the basis of differences or opposition, because "the like is unaffected by the like" (A 92). For example, when we touch, we can feel the cold via the warmth of our hand, when we taste, we experience sour via sweet, and vice versa; when we look, we do not distinguish by the same colours, but by dissimilar ones. Since perception functions based on experiencing differences, it is always to some extent painful. Pain is realised only at very intense sensations, for example, with bright colours or too much noise.

Regarding the relationship of the senses and cognition, we encounter a scarcity of resources that would allow us to reconstruct Anaxagoras' doctrine sufficiently.

It is obvious that he distinguished reality in "Parmenides' manner," to the visible (apparent) and invisible (unapparent) sphere. The true nature of reality cannot be ascertained solely on the basis of the senses: "Because of ... weakness [of the senses], we are not able to discern the truth" (B 21). The reason for this is that the abilities of the senses for grasping are limited, for instance, with regard to very small things or seeds. This is clarified by the following example: "For if we take two colours, black and white, then we pour one drop by drop into the other, the sight will not be able to discern the gradual changes, even though they take place in reality" (B 21). As we are unable to see the changes in the mixture arising from the gradual addition of drops of white to black, our senses cannot say anything to us about the process of mixing seeds that takes place at the microscopic level. This limitation may be the cause of our faulty assumptions, such as those related to the nature of creation and destruction. Therefore, it is believed that if reality can be known, it is through reason (*nous*) in particular. But despite of what has been said, according to some authors, Anaxagoras does not completely reject the senses as, "appearances are a vision of the invisible (*adelon*)" (B 21a). With the invisible, but real, we encounter particularly through phenomena; visible is the result of invisible homoiomeres and Reason, which are inaccessible to our senses. This could suggest that knowledge is possible only through the interplay of the senses and reason.

5. The Presocratic Atomists

We do not know much about the life of the Greek atomists, Leucippus (5th century BC) and Democritus (approx. 460 – 370). Democritus came from Abdera, as well as the sophist Protagoras. Today, it is not quite possible to adjudicate the exact share of individual authors in the formulation of atomistic theory. It is possible that Leucippus elaborated the overall character, while Democritus developed it for specific areas of interest. Curiously, most of the fragments we have first-hand are about the ethics of Democritus.[14] In ontology and natural inquiries we are to a much greater extent dependent on the reports and comments of later authors.

---

14 Although their authenticity is doubtful, a considerable number among them have been preserved under the name Democrates (Ricken, 1999, 37).

5.1. Atoms and Void

In the spirit of Pre-Socratic pluralism, atomists also respond to Eleatic philosophy by attempts to reconcile some moments of their concept of existence with the way we experience reality. In accordance with Parmenides, they argue, therefore, that coming to be and perishing do not exist. Since it is impossible that something was created from nothing and something disappeared into nothing, there must be an eternal, permanent, and unchanging existence that is one. For Leucippus and Democritus, this characteristic carries an *atom*. Against the spirit of the Eleatic doctrine, they argue that the number of atoms is infinite and thus multiplicity does not deny or exclude rationality. An atom, according to them, is *replete, immutable, and internally inviolable*. The concept of the atom should therefore resolve the difficulties raised by Zeno's aporia. According to Zeno, the assumption of multiplicity leads to an infinite regress, in which it would be impossible to determine the basic unit of size, which would not be further divisible. It is possible, but not certain, that Democritus distinguished between so-called physical and mathematical divisibility. Things can be physically divided to the level of atoms, but the atoms themselves cannot be further subdivided. Zeno's argument is thus elegantly circumvented: although one can imagine something smaller than an atom (it may be divided in the mind, so to speak, "mathematically"), physically, atoms are the smallest possible units. Incidentally, etymology indicates this fact: *a-tomos*, literally means not divisible. Atoms are not mutually identical; they differ in *shape* (as the letters A and N), *arrangement* (NA and AN), and *position* (N and Z) (67 A 6).

In their ontology, and once again against the spirit of Parmenides, the atomists introduce *non-being (mé on)*. It is *void* or empty space. Since there are an infinite number of atoms with an infinite number of shapes, empty space is infinite as well. This consideration has another side: if space is infinite, but there are only a limited number of atoms, there would be a threat that they would disappear into space. Atomists held in ontology a strict determinism: "No thing happens in vain, but all things happen for a reason and from necessity" (67 B 2).

The movement of the atom has no origin; it goes on forever and is affected only by the movement of other atoms. They collide with one another and can rebound or be given shape, they can combine. So even according to Leucippus and Democritus, what is commonly called coming and ceasing to be is nothing more than the segregation and aggregation of basic elements, only this time, atoms. Atoms differ from each other by their weight, which varies depending on their size (shape). Their shape also affects the state of compound materials; for example, a fire has a spherical shape that causes the great unstableness of fire. The weight of compound things further depends on the density, in which the atoms are linked. Items are heavier if there is only a little empty space among atoms. If the atoms are linked together sparsely, for a change, things composed of them are lighter. Since there are an endless amount of atoms and they move in unlimited space, nothing precludes the notion that by the merging of atoms more than one cosmos is simultaneously created and exists (67 A 21).

The strict determinism of the motion of atoms has serious consequence in the fact that there is no need for a further guiding principle corresponding to Empedocles' Love and Strife, or Anaxagoras' *Nous*. At the same time, the necessity standing behind the movement of atoms makes their movement random. This does not deny determinism, but rather emphasises that atoms move "blindly;" they do not seek some predetermined purpose or aim (*telos*) (67 A 22).

5.2 Knowledge and Cognition

The theory of atoms brings substantial implications for the understanding of knowledge. According to Sextus Empiricus, Democritus is attributed a sceptical attitude for the suggestion of following a core principle that we are "cut off from reality" (68 B 6). In some instances, this opinion interlocks with previous thinking, but in many ways it brings new stimuli. In the work of Parmenides, we encounter the notion that grasping through the senses is deceptive and the true nature of reality may be grasped only through *logos*. Even Empedocles' analogy with painting and the mixing of colours analogy by Anaxagoras highlighted the inaccessibility of true reality, its components, and ordering forces to our perception. Similarly, in atomism, we find the splitting of reality to the visible (apparent) and invisible (unapparent), where the former is the subject of our current experience and the latter represents the atoms and empty space that are inaccessible to our eyes. In the context of knowledge, two issues stand out that need to be distinguished. First, what encourages us to adopt the principle that we are cut off from reality? Secondly, what are the consequences of the atomistic ontology for knowledge and learning, or how does it explain them?

Regarding the principle of our separation from reality, atomists and Democritus in particular could be led by the relativisation of grasping through the senses, resulting in a certain scepticism about the possibility of ascertaining the truth. Aristotle believes that Democritus stemmed from a diverse and contradictory experience of the same thing:

"Furthermore, many of the other animals perceive in a way contrary to what we perceive, and the same animals do not always make the same sensory judgements. Thus it is unclear which judgements are true and which false. For no set of judgements is more true than another, but both are alike. That is why Democritus say either nothing is true, or at any rate it is unclear to us what is true" (68 A 112).

Since the same thing can be perceived differently – Democritus concludes – the senses do not give us any certain knowledge. For example, to a sick person, something can taste bitter, while to a healthy person, the taste is sweet. If the same thing appears differently to different persons, one cannot say what is in reality based on the senses (KRS 527-528), whether the thing is really sweet or bitter. In contrast to this "obscure cognition" (*gnoses skotie*), Democritus consequently defines genuine cognition (*gnoses gnesie*): "Of cognition there are two kinds, one legitimate (*gnesie*), one bastard (*skotie*). Of the bastard kind are these: sight, hearing, smell, taste, touch. And there is legitimate kind, which is distinct from the latter" (68 B 11).

Obscure cognition is an appearance at most. In contrast, genuine cognition is rational and leading, so to speak, "beyond" our sensory experience. This means that the apparent or obvious may not be taken as true in itself, as it must be clarified by something unapparent, but accessible to reason. This is exactly the function of atoms and empty space, which are, as opposed to experienced things, real:

> "Democritus sometimes rejects what appears to the senses and maintains that none of these appears

in truth, but only to opinion, but truth in existent things consists of there being atoms and the void" (68 B 125).

"The first principles of the universe are atoms and empty space; everything else is merely thought to exist (*nenomisthai*)" (DL IX, 44).

Therefore, Democritus applies atomistic principles to explain the progress of sensory perception, which he explains as atoms encountering our sensory organs. For example, eyesight functions as follows:

"Democritus says see is the reception of an image from things seen. The image is the form appearing in the pupil, and likewise in other transparent media that retain an image in them. He and before him Leucippus and after him the Epicureans held that certain apparitions flowed off objects from which they come, being effluences isomorphic with them (and these are visible things) so as to impinge on the eyes of seers and thus to produce sight" (67 A 29).

According to Democritus, sensory perception results from encounters of atoms that flow like effluences from things and our body organs. Therefore, Aristotle notes that Democritus reduces all perception to "touch" (68 and 119). The emitted atoms must touch our bodies, regardless of whether it is the sight, hearing, or touch; otherwise perception does not occur. This understanding of sensory perception thus represents a human as a being who is not isolated from the rest of nature and who is not a disinterested observer. On the contrary, we ourselves are composed of atoms and we are already immersed in the flow of atoms, so we are necessarily exposed to them: "In reality, we understand nothing securely, but we perceive what changes in relation to the disposition of the body as things enter or resist" (68 B 9). Democritus in this way identifies the origin of our assumptions and delusions.

Separation from reality, which finds its justification in the influence of atoms escaping the senses, led Democritus to a distinction between qualities existing in true sense and those that exist only as experienced in perception or by the "custom," convention (in modern times, J. Locke talked about the so-called primary and secondary qualities): "For by convention ... sweet, by convention bitter, by convention hot, by convention cold, by convention colour, but in reality atoms and void" (68 B 125). The real (primary) qualities of atoms are only their shape (size), location, etc. In contrast, (secondary) qualities like colour and taste exist only in perception, but not in reality. The atom is not red or blue, or sweet or hot, no such characteristic belongs to it (68 A 125). It is the nature of atoms that induce their perceived qualities in us. For example, the atoms with a smooth surface cause the perception of the colour white and black is caused by atoms with a rough surface (68 A 126).

It is the same with taste: a sharp (sour) taste is caused by a sharp shape of the atom; a sweet taste is caused by a rounded and large shape (68 A 129). In the distinction of real and experienced qualities, we may observe the explicit criticism of Anaxagoras. According to his view, all properties should be contained in homoiomeres in advance.

A sharp distinction between genuine and obscure knowledge and the relativisation of perception can guide us to the adoption of a hasty assumption that it is possible to cognise only if we isolate and cut off our thinking from all that is offered to us by our eyes or ears. But it seems that Democritus does not completely refuse the role of perception in learning. We may prove it by the famous "complaint of the senses:" "Wretched mind, after taking from us [senses] your evidence, do you overthrow us? Our fall will be your defeat" (68 B 125). It is obvious that we cannot rely completely on the senses. Thus, we face the question: if the senses are deceptive, what positive role can they play in cognition? In fragment B 125, the senses accuse the reason that it drew from them the evidence for its conclusions and that right after Democritus did not ascribe the real status to experienced qualities and instead he argues that they exist out of habit. Nevertheless, the positive role of perception can be twofold: firstly, as mentioned above, diverse and dissenting experience reminds us of the falsity of our assumptions, if they benefit only from experience. Secondly, our perception is not random, but it is always the result of the influence of invisible and unapparent atoms. So perception is a certain way to indirectly encounter the inevitable influence of atoms.[15] Thus, Anaxagoras' "appearances are a vision of the invisible" (B 21a) may be applied to Democritus as well.[16] The role of the senses in cognition, therefore, is the validation of our rational views (KRS 530), i.e. to provide evidence of the existence of atoms, empty space and their influence.

5.3 The Ethics of Democritus

While issues and solutions of the atomistic ontology fall within the framework of Pre-Socratic philosophy, the spirit of Democritus' ethics is rather closer to the classical period of Greek thinking. Even today, it is an important issue, to what extent and whether it is possible at all to reconcile these areas of concern. Democritus' eth-

---

15 In one of his "residential lectures" regarding dark knowledge, Jan Patočka observes: "While *Skotié gnómé* shows us things that are, and in a sense also, as they are. For example, when we see colours, or when we taste things, all this is very variable and imprecise ... And yet a colour reflects something of the nature of things, as well as taste" (Patočka, 1999, 217).

16 Sextus Empiricus adds to this quote from Anaxagoras: "and Democritus approves his opinion."

ics are individualistic, focused on the individual and the question of how to live a proper life. This does not deny their social dimension. On the contrary, Democritus also has something to say about a human's relationship to others. The aim of life is *euthymia*, "cheerfulness" or "contentment" (Suvák 2008, 35), and is associated with satisfaction. The core of ethics is to estimate the measure, the extent of our own capabilities and the options that a person must not exceed:

> "One who would be content (*euthymeisthai*) must not undertake too many tasks, either in private or in public life, nor go beyond his ability and his strength (*hyper te dynamin ... kai fysin*) in whatever he undertakes; but he must so keep guard that when fortune befalls and tempts him to excess in his judgement, he will set it aside and not take on more than he can handle. For right quantity is more secure than a huge quantity" (68 B 3).

An emphasis on our own limitations, however, is not just well meant advice or moralism in the manner of a folk proverb, but it raises important philosophical ideas. The first is the uplifting of the ideal of *knowledge of oneself*, of one's own nature (*physis*), which is associated with the recognition of one's own *measure* in private and public activities. A person who knows him/herself knows how big of a burden he/she may take on his/her shoulders without doing one's self damage. The second is the effort to prevent or minimise the role of chance or luck (*tyche*) in our lives. Luck can bring many benefactions in life, but they are given by chance: what it gives, chance may also take away. As long as one gets used to these benefactions, in the future may suffer their loss. Chance in Greek thought often acts in opposition to knowledge or art (*techne*).[17]

The aim of art is to provide life with an assurance and exclude our lives as far as possible from the influence of *tyche*. Democritus' sense of ethics in this sense is the art of life and it is named *wisdom*. A wise person is characterised by a good mind, because he/she prudently recognises his/her own peace and does not rely on chance. In contrast, the foolish live recklessly and let chance rule over them, which causes them suffering. The cause of suffering and evil in life, therefore, is the absence of knowledge: "Senseless people are shaped by the profits of chance (*tes tyches*), people aware of this things by the profit of wisdom" (68 B 197). Wisdom manifests in conscious choice among the various pleasures to avoid what does not bring benefit to a person: "Do not enjoy any pleasure which does not benefit" (68 B 72). Therefore, we can attribute a moderate hedonism to Democritus. *Euthymia* consists in moderation that also results in self-sufficiency and independence. Pleasures in life should be chosen according to their usefulness. The wise (*sophos*),

---

17 Cf. Suvák 2008, 34-35.

who is moderate, is independent, because he/she is not bound by the dominion of chance. On the contrary, folly is manifested by the ignorance of measure in what is beneficial and what is not.

6. The Sophists

The word "sophist" sounds to modern ears rather defamatory, rather than as an attempt to imply serious reflection. But the Greek word *sofistés* in the 5th century was a rather neutral term and generally referred to anyone who knew specific, significant knowledge. It is no surprise that the sophists as vocational teachers received this designation as their own. The idea of a sophist as a "professional liar," who misused skills for his/her own enrichment, is mainly a legacy of Plato and Aristotle. The Sophists opened new topics and transferred emphasis to new areas with the person at the centre of their interest. Even past thinking thematised the relationship between a person and the world and opened the door to the criticism of human capabilities to adequately perceive and cognise. Sophists increased these tendencies even further.

6.1 The Historical Context of Sophists

The rise of sophists, which can hardly be described as a single movement, is inextricably linked to the development of democracy. On one hand, democracy greatly expanded the possibilities of individual citizens to participate in government and the administration of common affairs. On the other hand, major offices should be designated to distinguished, appropriate individuals who excel over others, regardless of their origin. In the words of Pericles' famous funeral speech: "Our constitution is called a democracy because conduct of affairs is entrusted not to a few but to the many... [B]ut public preferment depends on individual distinction and is determined largely by merit..." (Thuc. 2.37). The basis of political success in a democracy is to be prowess, by which the individual stands out over others and this opens the door to the office. Although the influence of sophists cannot be linked exclusively with Athens, it is here, where they find the space for exertion that consisted in teaching prowess and the ability to succeed in public life. Thus, Protagoras in Plato's eponymous dialogue claimed that he would teach his student "good judgement (*euboulia*) ... in the affairs of his own city, showing how he may have most influence on public affairs both in speech and in action" (Plat. *Prot.* 318e-319a).

In light of the political framework it is no surprise that *rhetoric* provided a solid part of sophistic teaching and the problems of *speech* constituted the core interest of sophistic reflections. The function and importance of speech in the political sphere were also highlighted by Pericles: "We are all involved in either the proper formulation or at least the proper review of policy, thinking that what cripples action is not talk, but rather the failure to talk through the policy before proceeding to the required action" (Thuc. 2.40).

Public debate in democracy performs a critical function that provides space for the mutual confrontation of different views presented in speeches. Thereby, the ability to convince others of the appropriateness of an opinion becomes a key requirement for success in public life. Sophists therefore focused on issues of argument, possibilities to contest the position of another party, and to make better arguments. "Speech is a great potentate," wrote Gorgias in the *Encomium of Helen,* "who by means of tiniest and most invisible body achieves the most godlike results" (82 B 4).

But rhetoric, and particularly eristics as the art to litigate, is based on insights that carry a philosophical core. The emphasis on speech and language problems is closely related to the problem of the viability of human abilities in relation to the truth, whereby sophists picked up on earlier authors. For example, even in the works of Parmenides we could encounter some scepticism about human abilities to ascertain the truth based on experience. Parmenides in his poem explicitly distinguished from the area of truth revealed by thinking and the area of appearances where cognition is not possible. Gorgias, as we shall see, tried to go further and challenged the legitimacy of this distinction without permitting a safe return to immediate experience.

6.2 Protagoras of Abdera

The most famous contribution of Protagoras (about 490-420) was his relativistic argument, *homo mensura*, from the beginning of his treatise, *Truth*, which reads: "Of all things the measure is the man, of things that are that/how (*hos*) they are, of things that are not that/how (*hos*) they are not" (80 B 1). The potential relativism of this statement is obvious; it entails the conclusion that it is the person who finally decides on being and non-being of things. Protagoras' relativism is evident from his teachings about argument. According to Seneca, "Protagoras says it is possible to argue every position pro and con with equal plausibility – including the very question whether every position can be argued pro and con" (80 A 20).

Ontologically and epistemologically, Protagoras via *homo mensura* turns against the Eleatic separation of the areas of being and truth from the area of mere appearance and opinion. In a fragment (discovered in 1968) of Didymus of Alexandria, it is argued that "the being of things that are consists in being manifest." Thus, Protagoras argues against Parmenides that there is no difference between appearance and being. This obviously has an impact on the distinction between thinking and grasping existence and opinion based on the mutual imposing of theses about being and non-being that appear to the sophists as unfounded, because being is such as it appears to a person.

The statement of *homo mensura* is accompanied by several important controversies. For example, it is questionable how we should understand the word *hos*, which can be translated as both the conjunction "that" and the expression "as." The relationship between the person who perceives and intends, and the manner of being of things, is at stake here. The first option (translation of *hos* as "that") allows for a more radical interpretation, because in a way, it puts a person into the position of the arbiter of what exists and what does not. In contrast, the second option appears to leave things to their being, and a person is the measure of "only" how things appear. For both versions tight interpretations may be stipulated, in which even the ancient commentators were of different opinions.

Protagoras derives from the analysis of sensory experiences in relation to an appearing object. He could build on the example of wind, which two people experience differently (Plat. *Theaet.* 152a-c). The same wind can be felt as cold by one person, but someone else may feel it as warm or as not cold. Since things are as they appear in regard to people, both contradictory claims that arise from experience are true.

Despite the relativistic consequences of claims resulting from experience, the *ratio* of Protagoras' argument may be based on some *certainty* of the sensory input. The reason for this position is found in Plato's dialogue, *Theaetetus*. If two people experience the same object differently, there is no reason to think that one of them was wrong in the experiencing: "his food appears and is bitter to the sick, but appears and is the opposite of bitter to the man in health. Now neither of these two is to be made wiser than he is ... nor should the claim be made that sick man is ignorant because his opinions are ignorant, or the healthy man wise because his are different..." (Plat. *Theaet*. 166e). Perception does not deceive the sick person when he/she perceives the object as bitter in his/her state; nor does it provide false information if a person perceives the object as sweet when they are healthy, whereby the sensual experience provides unquestioned basis. Note the difference from Democritus. According to him, while on the basis of the contradictory experience of the same thing, we cannot say how it is. In fact, according to Protagoras, both options are true.

The statement of *homo mensura* does not regard only perception,[18] but it is meant to explain the relationship

---

18 According to A. Graeser, the quote *homo mensura* " is governed by paradigm of perceptive assertion" (2000 Graeser, 27).

between *opinion and its objects*. Protagoras based his opinion on a different understanding of the righteous and good in various communities. Again, righteous is what appears as righteous in that community, consequently what is regarded as righteous: "For I claim that whatever seems right and honourable to a city, is really right and honourable to it, so long as it believes it to be so" (Plat. *Theaet*. 167c). Apart from the context of law and politics, it is obvious that in this respect too, we meet with criticism of Parmenides' distinctions. According to Protagoras, it is not possible to separate truth and opinion. He hints that something true may appear only in opinion and by means of opinion, not outside this framework.

Against this background, Protagoras attempted to defend sophistic knowledge (*techne*) and its importance for the community, in which he based his position on the analogy of sophist's praxis and medicine. Despite the fact that our perceptions do not lie and are equal in this sense, Protagoras could attribute different values to individual perceptions.[19] Value is not based on the possibility of influencing the objective nature of the thing more adequately or true, but it depends on the criteria of the *usefulness* or *benefit* for someone and his condi-

---

19 In this context, in Theaetetus' dialogue bad perceptions as opposed to beneficial, healthy, and true perceptions are mentioned (Plat. *Theaet*. 167b-c).

tion. The aim of medicine is to change an unfavourable condition of the sick body to a healthy and beneficial state. Without Plato mentioning it, we can even assume that the physician does not convince the sick that his/her perception is wrong; on the contrary, certain perceptions may proclaim the symptoms, from which the physician may work out the treatment. However, if the doctor changes the status of a person through drugs, the doctor changes the content of perception. Therefore, the healed person cannot perceive the same in a like manner as before. Analogously, the role of a sophist consists in a change of opinion in the community via speeches, so that what the community considered not to be beneficial shall appear contrarily after a change of opinion.

The controversial statement in the treatise, *On the Gods,* is also interesting as Protagoras faced the condemnation of impiety because of it: "Concerning the gods, I cannot ascertain whether (*hos*) they exist or whether (*hos*) they do not, or what form they have; for there are many obstacles to knowing, including the obscurity of the question and the brevity of human life" (80 B 4). Its philosophical controversy lies in the fact that his relationship to the argument of a person as a measure is not obvious. At first glance, it seems that Protagoras does put himself into the position of one of the reasoning parties, but he goes beyond them, because he refers to the obstacles that make it impossible to say whether gods exist or not.²⁰ Note that there is a difference compared to the text of *homo mensura*: according to this approach, the gods exist for those who take the opinion that they exist, and by contrast, they do not exist for those who intend the opposite. But Protagoras refuses the demands of both sides. The statement of *homo mensura* may be applied at a higher level. The problem here would not be the argument in favour of the existence or non-existence of gods, but rather the inability to provide evidence for any of the parties, since there is no such evidence obvious to Protagoras. The counterparty of discourse at this level can only be someone who relies on the patency of the evidence in favour of or against their existence.²¹

6.3 Gorgias

Even Gorgias of Leontini (483-375) tries to undermine the eligibility of the Eleatic distinction of the areas of being and appearance, and eventually truth and illusion. His attack, however, is more radical compared to Pro-

---

20 The more radical fragment (A23) comes from *Theaetetus* (162d-e): "Noble youth and elders, you sit around arguing to the masses by calling on the gods, about whom in my speeches and writing on them I refuse to speculate whether they are or they are not."

21 For an interesting insight on the religious aspects of the thought of Protagoras, see Suvák 2014.

tagoras. We may observe this in fragment B 26: "Being is obscure if it does not attain seeming, seeming is ineffectual if it does not attain being." For Protagoras, appearing is not only identified with being, but also with the truth. For Gorgias, the boundary between being and appearing is blurry. Gorgias does not attribute any truth to appearing, but only seeming (*dokein*). Thus seeming penetrates the very heart of being itself.

A key difference between these thinkers emerges in the differences of their strategies against Eleatic and post-Eleatic philosophy. Gorgias' major contribution to the history of thinking is represented in, *On Nature or the Non-Existent*, which was preserved in two abstracts by Sextus Empiricus and Pseudo-Aristotle. In it, he tries to prove three well-known theses: 1. Nothing is; 2. Even if it exists, it is incomprehensible to man; and 3. Even if it is comprehensible, it surely cannot be expressed or communicated to another. At first sight, these theses attract by their alleged absurdity and many interpreters often see their reasoning as a rhetoric and eristic exercise. However, there are reasons to take them seriously, especially because they demonstrated the significant weaknesses of philosophical thought until that time. While Protagoras' criticism was based on the paradigm of sensory perception, Gorgias' is directly based on the dialectical argumentation style of Parmenides and Zeno, but in order to prove exactly the opposite of the Eleatic position.

6.3.1 Thesis I: "Nothing is"

Via the first thesis of "nothing is," the treatise, *On Non-Existence*, attacks the three ways of inquiry that Parmenides suggested. Gorgias then refutes the thesis that existence is, the argument that non-existence is, and ultimately the way of the two-headed. Since neither of these arguments is valid, he concludes "nothing is:" "if neither what-is nor what-is-not nor both together are, and nothing is conceivable but these, then nothing is" (82 B 3). Since the first and third ways were especially crucial for Parmenides and later philosophy, we will briefly focus our attention on them.

According to Gorgias, it is wrong to say that "being is," regardless whether we attribute it eternity or coming to be. The refutation of being which came to be functions exactly within Parmenides' intentions. Let us suppose that being came to be. If came to be, it could come to be either from being or non-being. The first option is questionable because "for if it is being, it did not come to be but already is" (82 B 3). But being also could not come to be from non-being, because it would have to participate in being, and therefore it would not be non-being. Therefore, even if being existed, it cannot come to be.

But Gorgias refuses to attribute eternity to being contrary to the spirit of Parmenides. This argument is also interesting as it is reminiscent and probably alludes to Zeno's aporia of space. If being is eternal, it has no beginning, and if it has no beginning, it is unlimited. According to Gorgias, the boundlessness of eternity also results in its non-being, because "it is nowhere" (82 B 3). He concludes this through the distinction between what is somewhere and wherein it is, or between the surrounded and the surrounding (as in Zeno's work, between what exists in space and space itself). If being exists somewhere, it will differ from wherein it is. However, since being is limitless, it may no longer be surrounded by anything else, so it does not exist anywhere.

Against the third way, namely the coexistence of being and non-being, Gorgias notes that he presupposes the being of non-being in regard to its being. So there is no difference between being and non-being, from which it is concluded that there is no being.

6.3.2 Thesis II: "Even if it exists it is incomprehensible to man"

The second thesis is clearly directed against Parmenides' identification of existence and thinking. This is already suggested by Gorgias' point of departure, "if the objects of thought are not things that are, what-is is not the object of thought" (82 B 3). He only needs to indicate that non-existent things are an object of thought. And if the object of thinking is non-being, being is beyond the possibilities of knowledge and understanding. The proof lies in thinking of fantasies:

"For if objects of thought are things that are, all objects of thought are, in just the way one thinks them, which is bizarre. For even if one thinks of a man flying or chariot racing in the sea, it does not immediately follow that the man is flying or the chariot racing in the sea" (82 B 3).

Note that Gorgias rejects the possibility of the distinction of objects of thinking into two kinds and relies on the absolute validity of one or the other possibility, because as being opposites, they are mutually exclusive: thought things either exist or do not exist. Therefore, if the first option is true, then we are inevitably led to the absurd conclusion that any idea, for example, a cart on sea, is an idea of something existing. However, if we may think of something non-existent, then the excluding contradiction between existence and non-existence makes it impossible for us to think of it existing.

However, if the aim of the treatise, *On Non-Existence*, was really to exploit the weaknesses of Eleatic philosophy against itself, then the criticism of the identification of existence and thinking is not as strong as the argument in the case of thesis I. Gorgias extends the concept of thinking so that it includes the objects of imagination (e.g. Scylla or Chimaira) which receives its material from experience. But in the context of Parmenides' poem, there is no indication that it would be legitimate.

6.3.3 Thesis III: "Even if it is comprehensible, it surely cannot be expressed or communicated to another"

Gorgias ties to prove this thesis in several steps. First, he relies on the fact that between speech and things that are to be known, there is a certain caesura, as there is between the senses, where for the eyesight, it is impossible to grasp sounds and hearing is unable to grasp colours. Speech, according to Gorgias, does not hand in the thing itself, if we grasp it by sensory perception: "For just as sight does not discern sounds, so hearing does not hear colours, but sounds. And speaker speaks, but not colours or objects... For, in the first place the speaker utters not a sound nor a colour but a speech, so that it is not possible to think a colour, but only to see it, nor to think a sound but to hear it" (Ps.-Arist. *MXG*. 980b1-8). Secondly, Gorgias turns against the possibility of knowledge that – so that we can talk about knowledge – must be one and the same with everyone who maintains it. Therefore, if it was possible to communicate something to another, knowledge is not possible, because the knowledge would exist in two persons at the same time and it would not be one. Thirdly, even if we recognise that the same knowledge exists in two persons, the same would appear differently for each of them, since both can be in different states, conditions, etc.

6.4 Physis and *nomos*

In the 5th century, the theme of the relationship between *physis* and *nomos* resonated strongly. For the sophists this relationship took the form of antitheses, according to which what is given by *physis*, it is not given by *nomos* and vice versa. The term *physis* roughly means "nature." The term *nomos* took on more layers in this period that do not contradict each other. It means both "usage or custom based on traditional or conventional beliefs as to what is right or true," or more specifically, "laws formally drawn up and passed, which codify 'right usage' and elevate it into an obligatory norm backed by the authority of the state" (Guthrie 2003, 57). Herodotus was one of those who drew attention to the deep-rootedness of *nomoi*:

> "When Darius was king, he summoned the Greeks who were with him and asked them what price would persuade them to eat their fathers' dead bodies. They answered that there was no price for which they would do it. Then he summoned those Indians who are called Callatiae, who eat their parents, and asked them (the Greeks being present and understanding by interpretation what was said) what would make them willing to burn their fathers at death. The Indians cried aloud, that he should not speak of so horrid an act."

Therefore a habit, Herodotus ascertains in reference to the poet Pindar, is "king of all" (Hdt. *Hist.* 3.38).

The diversity of *nomoi* is artificial, and is thus implicitly opposed to *physis*, which is universal and its rules are necessary. Sophists did not see the relationship of *physis* and *nomos* consistently. The diversity and deep-rootedness of nomoi *points* to the possibility that, in the end, it is a person who decides what *physis* is. In contrast, for the later sophists the belief that laws of communities are fraud against human nature shall not be an exception at all.

We could consider Protagoras (Graeser 2000, 37-38) the representative of the social conventions supremacy over nature, in whom we encounter the opinion that the community is the measure of what is just and good. But the myth, by which Plato conveys his position in *Protagoras* (320c-328d), suggests a more complex view. Humans differ from other animals, because they are – as spoken by Arnold Gehlen – deficient beings. Other animals have natural means for their self-defence and protection against weather. Compared with them, humankind is naked and thus faces natural inhospitability by designing tools. This necessity thus leads people to the discovery of art *(techne)*, by which they develop tools and dwellings. But since people are still not familiar with the political art of living in the community, the human race is dying partly because of the conflict with each other and because of an inability to unite against attacks of carnivores. Therefore, Zeus gives a person shame (*aidos*)[22] and justice (*dike*). But while other *technai* are subject to the division of labour, and not everyone has the same abilities, almost everyone receives and is endowed with gifts for political art from Zeus. The sense of this freely reproduced myth may be seen in the background of Protagoras 'attempt to defend the status of the teacher of virtue (*arête*). This would not be possible if we possessed virtue only by nature. At the very most, we receive only the gift for proficiency, which is achieved through education and instruction: "Instruction requires natural ability and practice (*fyseos kai askeseos*)" (80 B 3). In favour of learnability of virtue, according to Protagoras, speaks the fact that a punishment does not make sense if it is followed by satisfaction, but, above all, it aims for amendment that prevents future misconduct.

For later sophists, *nomos* often takes on a negative meaning. Antiphon's is a very interesting view. According to him, the justice contained in the standards of a community is often contradictory to human nature, prescribing to seek the beneficial and to avoid the unwholesome (Graeser 2000, 89). "Thus man would use justice in a way most advantageous to himself if, in

---

22 The term *aidos* is an ambiguous term, for which we have no appropriate equivalent and "manifests itself as what you express by thoughtfulness, friendliness, sense of decency, respect, humility, loyalty and respect for others" (Porubjak 2010, 87).

the presence of witnesses, he held the laws in esteem, whereas when he was alone, he valued the works of nature" (87 B 44). Antiphon emphasised that the laws of communities often cause damage to just people, for example, when suffering from injustice and holding to the belief that they should not recompense it in the same way. It is possible that Antiphon's intention is not to reject the laws of the community as such, but to highlight human nature as the critical standard for their assessment. Therefore, laws and customs should not go against nature, but should be harmonised with it.

Finally, the opposition between *physis* and *nomos* may be viewed in the reflection of religion. The above passage by Herodotus refers to the close interrelatedness of religious beliefs and norms of society. In this spirit, so to speak, later sophists turn the fragment of Heraclitus upside down, according to which "human laws are nurtured by the one divine law" (22 B 114). So, for example, Prodicus sees the psychological origin of religious beliefs in the usefulness of things and natural phenomena that people project as gods. The same psychological attitude is also found in Crito, for whom the closeness between the standards of community and religious formation are particularly significant. As with Antiphon, according to Crito, the effort to maximise one's own benefit may lead people to follow laws if they are in the public eye, but also to their violation in secret. Belief in gods is a ubiquitous human invention that arises from the need to compel criminals violating the norms in secret to obey the laws of the community. Therefore, the aim of religion is, according to Crito, primarily to prevent the violation of laws through the fear of a being with superhuman knowledge, for whom nothing remains hidden.

List of Abbreviations

DL = Diogenes Laertius: *Lives of Eminent Philosophers*

Hdt. *Hist.* = Herodotus: *The Persian Wars*

KRS = Kirk, G. S., Raven, J. E., Schofield, M.: *Předsókratovští filosofové*

Plat. *Crat.* = Plato: *Cratylus*
Plat. *Prot.* = Plato: *Protagoras*
Plat. *Theaet.* = Plato: *Theaetetus*

Ps.-Arist. *MXG.* = Pseudo-Aristotle: *On Melissus, Xenophanes and Gorgias*
Simpl. *In Phys.* = Simplicius: *In Aristotelis Physica commentaria*

Thuc. = Thucydides: *The Peloponesian War*

Bibliography

Cooper, J. M., Hutchinson, D. S. (eds.): *Plato. Complete Works.* Indianapolis, Ind.: Hackett Publishing1997, 101-156.

Diogenes Laertius: *Lives of Eminent Philosophers. Volume I. Books 1-5.* Cambridge, Mass.: Harvard University Press 1972.

Graeser, A.: *Řecká filosofie klasického období.* Praha: Oikoymenh 2000.

Graham, D. W.: *The Texts of Early Greek Philosophy. Part I.* Cambridge: Cambridge University Press 2010.

Graham, D. W.: *The Texts of Early Greek Philosophy. Part II.* Cambridge: Cambridge University Press 2010.

Guthrie, W. K. C.: *The Sophists.* Cambridge: Cambridge University Press 2003.

Herodotus: *The Persian Wars. Volume II. Books 3-4.* Cambridge, Mass.: Harvard University Press 1995.

Hussey, E.: *Presokratici.* Praha: Petr Rezek 1997.

Hussey, E.: Pythagoreans and Eleatics. In: Taylor, C. C. W. (ed.): *Routledge History of Philosophy. Volume I. From the Beginning to Plato.* London: Routledge 2003, pp. 128-174.

Kahn, Ch. H.: Appendix I. In: *Anaximander and the Origins of Greek Cosmology.* New York: Columbia University Press 1960, pp. 219-230.

Kahn, Ch. H: *The Art and Thought of Heraclitus.* Cambridge: Cambridge University Press 2001.

Kirk, G. S., Raven, J. E., Schofield, M.: *Předsókratovští filosofové*. Praha: Oikoymenh 2004.

Kočandrle, R.: *Fysis iónských myslitelů. Rozprava nad peripatetickou dezinterpretací*. Červený Kostelec: Pavel Mervart 2008.

Kratochvíl, Z.: *Délský potapěč k Hérakleitově řeči*. Praha: Herrmann & synové 2006.

Osborne, C.: Heraclitus. In: Taylor, C. C. W. (ed.): *Routledge History of Philosophy. Volume I. From the Beginning to Plato*. London: Routledge 2003, 88-128.

Palmer, J.: Parmenides.[online]. In: Zalta, E. N. (ed.): *Stanford Encyclopedia of Philosophy*, Summer 2012, URL: <http://plato.stanford.edu/archives/sum2012/entries/parmenides/>, [2014-12-07].

Parry, R.: Empedocles. [online]. In: Zalta, E. N. (ed.): *Stanford Encyclopedia of Philosophy*, Fall 2012, URL: <http://plato.stanford.edu/archives/fall2012/entries/empedocles/>, [2015-01-13].

Patočka, J.: *Nejstarší řecká filosofie*. Praha: Vyšehrad 1996.

Patočka, J.: *Platón a Evropa*. In: *Péče o duši II*. Praha: Oikoymenh 1999.

Porubjak, M.: *Vôľa (k) celku. Človek a spoločenstvo rečou Homéra a Theognida*. Pusté Úľany: Schola Philosophica 2010.

Ricken, F.: *Antická filosofie*. Olomouc: Nakladatelství Olomouc 1999.

Suvák, V.: Etické myslenie v predsokratovskom období. In: Remišová, A. (ed.): *Dejiny etického myslenia v Európe a USA*. Bratislava: Kalligram 2008, pp. 23-41.

Suvák, V.: Prótagorovi bohovia. In: *Filosofický časopis*, Vol. 62, No. 5, 2014, pp. 661-673.

Thucydides: *The Peloponesian War*. Oxford: Oxford University Press 2009.

Vítek, T.: *Empedoklés I. Studie*. Praha: Herrmann & synové 2001.

Vlastos, G.: *Studies in Greek Philosophy. Volume I: The Presocratics*. Princeton, NJ: Princeton University Press 1996.

Michal Zvarík works as a lecturer at the Department of Philosophy at Faculty of Philosophy and Arts, Trnava University. His research interests include ancient Greek philosophy, Hannah Arendt and phenomenology, mostly in relation to phenomena of a political space. In present he is providing research on intellectual virtues in Aristotle, especially on the problem of phronesis. In 2011 he published Predsudok vo fenomenológii každodennosti: *Štruktúra predsudku u Edmunda Husserla, Alfreda Schütza a Martina Heideggera* and in 2013 co-translated Home & Beyond: *Generative Phenomenology after Husserl,* by Anthony Steinbock into Slovak.

Európska únia
Európsky sociálny fond

Európska únia

Operačný program
VZDELÁVANIE

VÝSKUMNÁ AGENTÚRA

www.ingramcontent.com/pod-product-compliance
Ingram Content Group UK Ltd.
Pitfield, Milton Keynes, MK11 3LW, UK
UKHW041228200426
11947UKWH00035B/575